Trinny Woodall & Susannah Constantine

what not to wear part 2

for every occasion

Trinny Woodall & Susannah Constantine
what not to wear
part 2

for every occasion

Photography by **Robin Matthews**

WEIDENFELD & NICOLSON

to Sten and Johnnie for their continued love and support

thanks

Susan and Jinny for their patience, inspiration and faith in us

Michael and Ed who without each other couldn't have us and the book

Charlotte for making the most of an ageing situation

Pookie for taking the concept of work experience to a new level

Zelda and Christiano for combing out our worries and our hair

Robin and Aitkin for making two old hags look vaguely respectable

David for being as wonderfully anal as Trinny

First published in the United Kingdom in 2003 by
Weidenfeld & Nicolson
An imprint of The Orion Publishing Group
Wellington House
125 Strand
London WC2R OBB

Text copyright © Susannah Constantine & Trinny Woodall 2003
Design and layout © Weidenfeld & Nicolson 2003

Photography by Robin Matthews

Hair by Zelda at Richard Ward Hair & Beauty, 162B Sloane St,
Knightsbridge, London SW1X 9BS
Make-up by Charlotte Ribeyro
Styling by Lucy Page

By arrangement with the BBC
The BBC logo is a trade mark of the British Broadcasting
Corporation and is used under licence.
BBC logo © BBC 1996
What Not to Wear logo © BBC 2002

The moral right of Susannah Constantine & Trinny Woodall to
be identified as the authors of this Work has been asserted in
accordance with the Copyright, Designs and Patents Act of 1988

A CIP catalogue record for this book is available from the
British Library

ISBN 0 297 84355 9

Design director David Rowley
Editorial director Susan Haynes
Designed by Clive Hayball and Austin Taylor
Edited by Jinny Johnson

Printed and bound in Italy

contents

In the first **What Not to Wear** book we laid down the rules of how to match the right clothes to **the most common figure faults**. This manipulation of the truth went a long way towards helping wipe out worry spots altogether. You'd think that such a clearly laid out, join-the-dots approach would leave no room for more words of wisdom. Well, while it goes a long way to eradicating tapered trousers and exposed mounds of mottled arm, there is still a vast area of '**what to wear when**' not catered for. It's all very well having big tits neatly encased in plummeting necklines and saddlebags disguised to the point of non-existence, but all this trickery can be utterly obliterated if you are **dressing inappropriately for the occasion**.

Sad though it is, there's no getting away from the fact that, these days, we are **judged by the way we look**. Some strong, secure, independent women say they couldn't care less about the opinions of others, but we know that they're lying through their teeth. Who in their right mind would rather be a wedding day embarrassment than the star guest in danger of **out-shining** the bride? And while you might not admit it, this feat would give you more of a lift than Prozac.

No matter what a woman's age, she is faced with a series of milestones, special events and occasions that all require careful dress planning. In **What Not to Wear Part 2**, we aim to guide the misguided into looking the part for all manner of life-changing moments. The book demonstrates how dressing well can help you get what you want. It will train those bound by what the neighbours say to break **free from stereotypes**. It will urge those who are lacking in confidence to go the extra mile in order gain that much needed self-belief to win the job, get the bloke or fit in with the sleek sophisticates oiled up on the beach in southern Spain. It will enable girls to make **dressing decisions on their own**, without the help of competitive peers, and make dates for those newly single exciting rather than excruciating.

The book appears to be offering **miracles** and in a sense it does. Nearly all women understand the horror of realising that you're wearing the wrong clothes. We are hot-wired to know that dressing suitably, **yet with individual flair**, will make us feel on top of the world, but so many of us just don't have the wherewithal to get there.

Were you aware that dressing head-to-toe in one designer label, complete with matching bag and shoes, may look coordinated but shows no **imagination** whatsoever? Are you privy to the secrets of not resembling a lobster in a bikini, even if you've burnt like one? Do you know how to win over a prospective boss or make **speedy transformations** from daytime workwear to evening glamour? Do you like being over- or underdressed at a party and are you happy shocking the priest at a church wedding?

The moral here is to consider the **occasion** more than yourself before deciding what look to opt for. If you do this, you're less likely to make a fool of yourself by turning up adorned in full-length mink at the Animal Rights convention. It's **rude and thoughtless** to arrive unkempt and shabby when your hostess has gone to great lengths. Think how upset you'd feel if your marquee was littered with guests wearing trainers and jeans when you had spent months and thousands creating a wonderland of elegance?

As important as the event is **what you want to achieve at that moment**. Don't be fooled into thinking your knight will want to ravage you when you're cloaked in velour, or an interviewer will be telepathic and see into your genius brain through a barbed armour of missing buttons and brothel-creeping shoes. You need to let your true **personality** shine through while respecting the nature of the event and being aware of how others might view you. If, for example, you're a lively, vital type, it's criminal to murder your spirit by over-matching. Uniform dressing is the quickest way to stamp out any individuality, while a little **risk taking** is the fast-track to getting noticed.

The most common dressing dilemmas are demonstrated in the book by showing what Miss and Mrs Average might wear versus the kind of cool adopted by Miss and Mrs Individual. On the left-hand pages you will see the most stereotypical fashion 'looks', adopted by women who are lost in choked lifestyles and have no time for clothes. Labelled with a big fat X, these outfits are **nondescript and have no impact**. Some of them may seem smart or even rather nice. Well, they could well be... for a different occasion, on your mother or in a bygone era.

The collection of outfits assembled on the right-hand pages and, yes, you guessed it, marked with a luscious 'tick', are there to be used as **yardstick solutions**. If you like the looks and have similar clothes and shapes to us, then go for them. If, however, you think we look like shit, adapt them to your own personality, shape and style. The **tone** of the outfits, rather than their exact composition, is what we hope to help you with. The looks can be varied by the amount of **accessorising** you apply. Your aim should be to stand out as a chic woman not look like the haberdashery counter at John Lewis.

Each chapter is defined by an occasion and most are divided into '**Smart, Casual and Trendy**' themes. Unless you are an old trout hankering after teenage years or a filly desperate for some premature sophistication, we assume that younger readers will veer towards the **trendy** looks and older babes will prefer the **smart** ones. Those who know their shape and how best to flatter it will quickly see that all the looks can be adapted to suit **different ages, sizes and budgets**. Casual has a foot in both camps and the outfits are adaptable for any age.

The '**What it says about you**' quote under each picture is like having a neutral friend whispering the truth on what your clothes say about you. It tells you that clothes can be more effective than you might think – both in a **positive and negative** way.

If you think we have turned occasion dressing into a science that needs to be studied for years as a post-graduate course, you couldn't be more wrong. Sure, it takes time to look great, but only from the point of **planning ahead**. If you have the dress, don't leave finding the crucial shoes to the last minute. Look at your clothes and work out which pieces are the **most adaptable** with a change of accessories. The best jacket, for example, is the one the girls envy when you wear it with jeans and a T-shirt, yet pulls blokes when the T-shirt is dropped and the jeans are replaced by a tight pencil skirt. A core wardrobe that works for your body shape can be added to and transformed. With this in mind, along with a little inspiration from within these pages, living with clothes can become hassle free and frivolous.

In **What Not to Wear 1** we aimed to wipe out the phrase 'does my bum look big in this'. With **Part 2** we'd love to eradicate the panic of 'I've got nothing to wear!' We so empathise with the agony of trying to look your best when the cupboard is bare or your staple seduction dress for some reason doesn't work on a Tuesday. It's sod's law that just when we're most rushed, or in need of looking our most spectacular, our clothes will let us down.

That's when you want your best friend, wardrobe-side, to advise you. But she may not be there when you most need her. She may also want to outdo you on the night. We are much more reliable, so think of us as your **best friends** instead. We may only be peering from these pages, but at least our advice is objective, always at hand and a damn sight cheaper than running out to buy a new outfit for every invitation that come through the letter box.

The information ahead is essential to those of you who want to **feel better about yourselves**. We know how much looking good can change a woman's whole outlook on life. If you look chic, not corporate, you'll perform better. If you look hip, you'll have more fun, and if you feel sexy you'll give better blow jobs! **So, girls, look fab** and get the man, the job, the promotion. Win the egg-and-spoon race and out-glitz the hostess at her own party! Most of all have a blast.

X

Sarah x

the interview Going for a job interview, no matter what your age or your know-how, is a terrifying experience. As important as your CV, if not more so, is your appearance. When you walk through that door, the inquisitionists will be looking out for dirty, bitten nails, polished shoes, stained clothes, a confident smile. They will be impressed by a positive disposition and assured responses to tricky questions. If you look like shit, you'll feel like shit and perform like a sub-being not worthy of breathing, let alone residing at the rarefied desk left vacant by 'the marvellous girl we had before'. Unfortunately there is no one solution to interview dressing needs. Your age, experience and the job you are after should definitely be reflected in the clothes you wear. A woman going back to work after her kids have flown will probably be more unsure of her talent than a fresh-faced graduate, so she needs to exude a power she may not feel. The student wants to convey enthusiasm mixed with a desire to commit and willingness to learn. Surely this can't be done with clothes? Oh, but it can. Because in the interview room you are what you wear.

the interview

1

first job

✗ The suit is predictable and lacks flair

Skirt is too short

Shirt is pretty but overpowered by the black

Too much make-up

Hair is too 'done'

Enormous bag is out of proportion with the outfit

what it says about you

'I show my legs to distract attention from a lack of grey matter and I'll be late every morning because I take too much time to do my hair. I'm up for a bit of overtime, if you know what I mean, so I know you'll give me the job.'

first job

✓ Entire look is clean and crisp

Trouser suit is more individual than a skirt suit

The accessories, though subtle, show flair and add to rather than detract from the feminine cut of the manly pinstripe

what it says about you

'I don't need fuss or frills because my CV speaks for itself. Being unthreatening yet confident, I'll fit in with both sexes in the office. You know I'm on the pulse because I've got a designer-inspired bag. I like being an individual and I'm ready to take on a challenge.'

first job

X Combats are too scruffy

Tailored denim jacket looks sloppy with the combats

Bare midriff not appropriate

Overall look demonstrates a cockiness and lack of personal care

what it says about you

'I'm dressing how I dress every day. I don't think I need to make any changes to the way I look, even for an interview. Take me as I am or not at all.'

first job

✓ The coat is a smarter way to wear denim

The trousers are not as casual as the combats but still fun

Trainers take on an air of respectability under longer trousers

what it says about you

'I have respect for myself and this job. I like to be comfortable as well as casually smart – but I won't come to the office looking like a slob.'

first job

✗ So of the moment, she can only be a fashion victim

High gold sandals are great for the disco but not the interview room

Everything is too tight so she looks tarty

the interview trendy

what it says about you

'I am a fashion sheep who spends all day reading glossy magazines and painting my toenails fuchsia pink. I'll work hard – when you're watching.'

first job

✓ **Dress over trousers looks modern but still smart enough for an interview**

The quirky accessories show personality

Trousers are the right length with the high, strappy shoes

what it says about you

'I'm creative with a sense of fun. I won't be scared to go out on a limb if I need to rise to a challenge in my job. I buy retro clothing to save money, which means I'll be loyal and work hard to get a pay rise.'

back to work

✗ **Loose long-line jacket is very dated**

Trendy accessories bear no relation to old-fashioned suit

Never wear matching accessories – shows you were a pushover with the sales assistant, who made you buy the 'set'

what it says about you

'I've been out of work for the last ten years and that was the last time I wore this suit. You may think me dull, but look how on the pulse I am with my matching bag and shoes.'

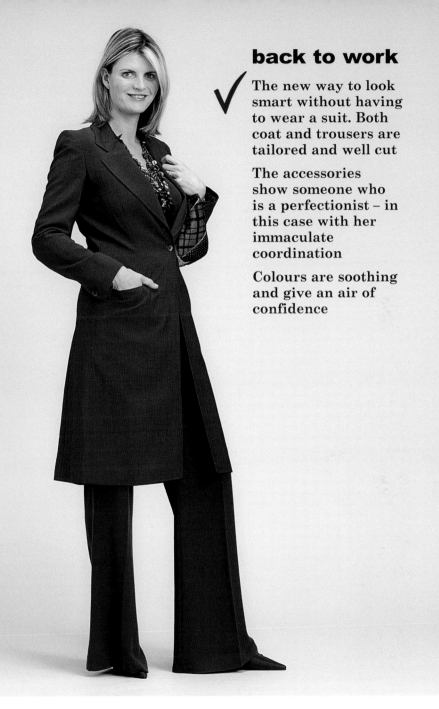

back to work

✓ The new way to look smart without having to wear a suit. Both coat and trousers are tailored and well cut

The accessories show someone who is a perfectionist – in this case with her immaculate coordination

Colours are soothing and give an air of confidence

what it says about you

'Over the last ten years I've taken time out to further my education. I'm very at ease with myself and others, and I'm able to handle any situation. I'm not desperate for work, but I do want to expand my skills.'

back to work

✗ Tapered trousers are
unflattering and too short
for the clumpy boots

Clothes look defensive and
as if she wears them every
day – no effort made

Shoulder pads show the
top to be a good friend
from the 80s

the interview casual

what it says about you

'I'm prim and proper but Jesus, am I dreary! There's not really
much point to me aside from the fact I'll be as reliable and as
exciting as the coconut matting on your doorstep.'

back to work

✓ Long cardigan is relaxed alternative to a jacket

Flared trousers are modern and far more flattering than tapered – and they're the right length for the shoes

A fitted shirt reveals the figure without being blatant

what it says about you

'It's true, I haven't worked for an age, but it's been great. Now I'm ready to fit in with a team and start a new phase of my life. Clothes aren't the be-all and end-all for me as I rely on my approachability to make friends.'

back to work

X Everything about this look is stiff

The hair is rigid and was last seen on Flight 001

Scarf is a desperate attempt to jolly up the funereal black

The shoes may be sensible, comfortable and practical, but they make feet look like soup plates

what it says about you

'I'm terribly efficient and very set in my ways. I don't have a life so I'll never be late – but I will bore the pants off everyone else in the office.'

back to work

✓ A dress over trousers is a contemporary look

Muted colours are un-flashy and warm

The bag is fun and a nod to the trend of the moment

Shoes are light and flattering

what it says about you

'I have a natural stylishness which will be reflected in my work. I'll fit in well with everyone and I have the makings of a future team leader.'

the interview/first job

	£	££	£££
smart	Oasis, Zara, Dorothy Perkins, Warehouse, Mango, Designers at Debenhams **Accessories** Accessorize, Mikey, Office, Nine West	Jigsaw, LK Bennett, Whistles, Karen Millen, Press & Bastyan, Coast, French Connection **Accessories** Jigsaw, Karen Millen, Furla, Coccinelle, Pied à Terre	Prada, Helmut Lang, Gucci, Roland Mouret, Vivienne Westwood, Chloé, Louis Vuitton, Paul and Joe, Joseph, Alexander McQueen, Armani, Ralph Lauren, Calvin Klein **Accessories** Hermès, Prada, Mulberry, Tods
casual	Warehouse, Zara, Gap, Topshop, Knickerbox, Dune, Dorothy Perkins, Oasis **Accessories** Gap, Accessorize	Nuala, Diesel, Miss Sixty, French Connection, Martin Kidman, Michael Stars, Bodas **Accessories** Nike, Puma, Whistles, Karen Millen, Jigsaw	Marc Jacobs, Marni, Brora, Juicy Couture, Chloé, Earl, Hogan, Tods, Prada Sport **Accessories** J&M Davidson, Stella McCartney, Luella @ Mulberry, Hogan, Tods, Marni
trendy	Oasis, Zara, Gap, Topshop, Knickerbox, Dune, H & M, Freedom @ Topshop, Mango, Pink Soda **Accessories** Oasis, Faith, Accessorize, Mikey	Jigsaw, Pied à Terre, LK Bennett, French Connection, Miss Sixty, Day Birger et Mikkelsen, Diesel, Pebble **Accessories** Agatha, Butler & Wilson	Rozae Nichols, Steinberg & Tolkien, Rellik, Marni, Seven, Juicy Couture, Joie, Anya Hindmarch, Prada, Miu Miu, Ann Louise Roswald, Chloé, Etro **Accessories** Anya Hindmarch, J&M Davidson, Jamin Puech, Buba, Scorah Patullo, Christian Louboutin, Swarovski, Sigerson Morrison

the interview/back to work

	£	££	£££
smart	Zara, Dorothy Perkins, Warehouse, Oasis, Designers at Debenhams **Accessories** Zara, Accessorize, Freedom @ Topshop, Office, Faith, Bertie, Mikey	French Connection, LK Bennett, Karen Millen, Reiss, Whistles, Jigsaw **Accessories** Butler and Wilson, Coccinelle, Billy Bag, Karen Millen, Russell & Bromley, LK Bennett	Joseph, Prada, Mulberry, Chloé, Paul and Joe, Wright and Teague, Celine, Alexander McQueen, Chanel, Ann Demeulemeester, Pringle **Accessories** Pippa Small, William Welsted, Celine, Erickson Beamon, Tods, Hermès, Prada, Wright and Teague, Sigerson Morrison
casual	Oasis, Marks & Spencer, Warehouse, Zara, H & M, Designers at Debenhams, Next, Knickerbox, Gap, Dune, Bertie **Accessories** Dune, Bertie, Designers at Debenhams, Next	French Connection, Whistles, Jigsaw, LK Bennett, Thomas Pink, Hobbs **Accessories** Furla, Coccinelle, Russell & Bromley, LK Bennett, Pied à Terre	Nicole Farhi, Joseph, Brora, Prada, Calvin Klein, Armani, Helmut Lang, Ralph Lauren **Accessories** Tods, Mulberry, Hermès
trendy	Oasis, Warehouse, Zara, Topshop, Gap, Dorothy Perkins, Laura Ashley **Accessories** Accessorize, Faith, Mikey, Freedom @ Topshop, Zara, Office	French Connection, Whistles, Jigsaw, Coast, Nuala, Reiss, Uth **Accessories** Russell & Bromley, Karen Millen, Whistles	Diane Von Furstenberg, Chloé, Joseph, Marni, Seven, Juicy Couture, Joie, Missoni, Allegra Hicks, Melissa Odabash **Accessories** Jamin Puech, Buba, Scorah Patullo, Sigerson Morrison

the interview

- Go on the Internet and find out some basic facts about the company. However low- or high-powered the position you're going for, some knowledge shows initiative and interest

- Think of something to ask your interviewer when you're asked if you have any questions

- Take a bath in rosemary oil to wake you up and make you feel more alert

- Make sure you have clean nails and clean shoes, and go easy on the make-up

- Do a stinky breath test with a friend

- Switch off your mobile phone!

- If the interviewer is scary looking, imagine him or her on the loo

- Give a firm handshake and look the interviewer in the eye

tips

work wear The work place is no different to any other environment when it comes to clothes. Even wearing a uniform doesn't give a woman the license to be predictable in how she looks. If you want to stay bland and in the background like an invisible worker bee, fine: stick to corny suits or pleated skirts. If, however, you want to rise through the company, oust the boss, remain in power or catch the eye of the office stud, then what you wear is vital. We aren't suggesting your wardrobe becomes a theatrical costume drama. Going overboard can be as detrimental as looking the part is beneficial. You need to dress for where you want to get in your job. A uniform of sorts takes away the pain of the morning what-to-wear decision, but it must be made particular to you without offending the boss or causing envy among your colleagues and titters within your workforce. Stylish accessories will set you apart from the crowd and make you feel a little special. This does wonders for your confidence, a feeling that will enhance the way you look and affect everything you do at work.

work
wear

2

the boss

✗ **Hard, severe suit gives an unapproachable feel**

Slicked hair with the angular jacket makes for an androgynous look

Skirt length is unflattering for all but the best of legs

what it says about you

'You mess with me and you are O.U.T. I don't like any competition in the boardroom or the bedroom. My career is my life so I only sleep with colleagues.'

the boss

✓ Softer lines while still retaining the 'boss' image

Kelly bag is an elegant alternative to a briefcase

Stylish, imaginative accessories show a woman who makes time for the finer things in life... like shopping

what it says about you

'I'm sympathetic to the needs of my employees, but I still command respect. I have another life beyond the office, which makes me more relaxed at work.'

the boss

✗ The look is sloppy and juvenile

Jeans are fine for casual work but only when worn as tailored trousers

Leave hooded tops at home or give them to your kid sister

Looks like the dog has got at the shoes

what it says about you

'I want to be one of the team and I like my employees to see me as an equal. I do what they do well but do I have the experience and know-how to do more?'

the boss

Even when casually dressed, the boss needs to show authority which the jacket implies

The flat shoes are good run-around-on-the-feet-all-day type of footwear

Hair is tidy and slick, giving the casual lines of the outfit an air of sophistication

what it says about you

'I'm a doer and happy to muck in. I'm in touch with my staff, but they all know why I am the boss so they'd never dream of overstepping the mark.'

the boss

✗ A plain black suit turns a look into a uniform

There are no details to make the outfit interesting

Nice for a city job, but for something more creative? We don't think so

what it says about you

'I'm boring and conservative. God knows how I made it into a hip work environment – let alone getting the opportunity to run one.'

the boss

✓ Demonstrates style and confidence

Not afraid to wear something a little different and stand out, but because the colours are neutral the look isn't too flashy

Belt shows a good eye for unique details

what it says about you

'I inspire my staff to work hard and I have a strong sense of personal initiative and creativity which shows in the way I look as well as in what I do.'

the executive

X Tweed suits look frumpy
unless they are very fitted

Heavy black accessories
weigh down and cheapen
a look

Flesh-coloured tights
should only be worn as
support stockings or to
control varicose veins

what it says about you

'I've been in this business for a long time so I know what
I'm talking about. That is, until a new client comes up
with some innovative ideas that I refuse to listen to.'

the executive

✓ Black looks great when worn in softer fabrics

Show off your figure. It will give you confidence

Wear fine fishnets – dead cool with open toes or boots

what it says about you

'I'm smart, sassy and know how to use my sexuality in a professional way to get new business. Looking good helps me to do my job well.'

the executive

X Long cardigan worn with the same length skirt shortens the torso

Pale shirt makes features look washed out

Heavy, old-fashioned shoes are highlighted by the skirt length

what it says about you

'I'm old before my time. I've worked myself into the ground and no longer have any enthusiasm for my job so I'm just going through the motions.'

the executive

Fitted sweater
with trousers looks
comfortable yet
practical

Wearing the same
colour top and bottom
lengthens the torso

Trousers are less
dating than a skirt

High heels add a touch
of glamour

what it says about you

'Frippery and frills detract from the job ahead, which
I take on in a relaxed yet determined fashion.'

the executive

X Wearing every trend of the season makes you look like you are obsessed with your appearance

Too much going on here but wearing just one key piece at a time would make it stand out

what it says about you

'I am a sad fashion victim who lives and breathes shopping. The only reason for working is to subsidise my addiction to clothes.'

the executive

A velvet skirt can look great during the day if teamed up with chunky leather boots

The nipped-in cut of the shirt shows off the figure

The shirt was bought as a key fashion piece but will become a classic, thanks to its shape

what it says about you

'Those in the know will appreciate my discerning eye for subtler trends. I don't need clothes that do the talking because I am more than capable of doing that myself.'

work wear trendy

41 | work wear 2

the pa

X Black and pastels don't do anything for each other

Pale lipstick entirely flattens any complexion

Just because the matching chain necklace and hoop earrings are gold doesn't make them classy or interesting

what it says about you

'I am timid so don't yell at me cos I'll cry. I'll arrive at work every day filled with the fear of doing something wrong, so I'll never think for myself.'

the pa

✓ Colours are subtle and
work well together

The look is unobtrusive
yet individual

The boots add height
but don't hinder
running around

A fabulous belt is more
exciting than lots of
gold jewellery

what it says about you

'I have flair, I'm sophisticated and confident. I won't try
to overpower my boss, but she'll always be proud of me.
When the boss is away, I run the office so well that no
one notices she's gone.'

the pa

✗ Sweatpants are taking the word 'casual' too far

No matter how laid back your job, you should always have clean hair

Zip top looks like weekend gym gear

Overall look says 'Sunday'

AURA SP

what it says about you

'I rolled out of bed and came straight into work. I do a lot of office gossiping – and sometimes a little work. I'm a bit of a slacker and my job is not a priority.'

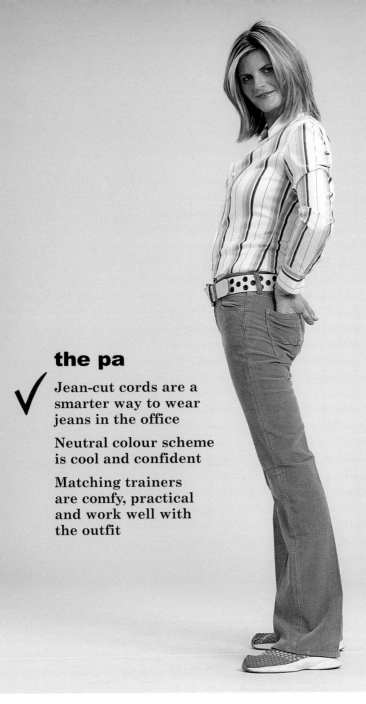

the pa

✓ Jean-cut cords are a smarter way to wear jeans in the office

Neutral colour scheme is cool and confident

Matching trainers are comfy, practical and work well with the outfit

what it says about you

'I'm a very efficient worker and I'm comfortable in my job. I stay on task, but I also know how to have a good time. Keep me in mind for a promotion and I promise you won't regret it.'

the pa

✗ Showing off a bare midriff at work is totally inappropriate

An evening top during the day only works if teamed with flat or chunky shoes

Belt is just overegging the pudding

Stilettos are impractical for someone who's running around all day

what it says about you

'I look available and I'll sleep with anyone to try and work my way up. There's certainly no other reason why I should ever be promoted.'

the pa

 The skirt is High Street and follows a trend

For height and practicality a wedge shoe works best at work

Looks smart but not like she's trying to outshine her boss

what it says about you

'I'm very aware of everything current. I know how to go far on a tight budget, which is a useful skill in my work. I'm young and energetic and ready for anything you want to throw at me.'

work wear/the boss

	£	££	£££
smart	Zara, Dorothy Perkins, Designers at Debenhams, Gap, Warehouse, Mango, Oasis, Principles **Accessories** Designers at Debenhams, Office, Bertie, Mikey, Freedom @ Topshop, Zara	Hobbs, Karen Millen, Michael Stars, Jigsaw, Press & Bastyan, LK Bennett, Bella Freud for Jaeger, Whistles **Accessories** Agatha, LK Bennett, Russell & Bromley, Butler and Wilson	Prada, Hermès, Gucci, Calvin Klein, Balenciaga, Chloé, Nicole Farhi, Ralph Lauren, Armani, Helmut Lang, Celine, Ann Demeulemeester, Michael Kors, Chanel **Accessories** Erickson Beamon, Hermès, Tods, Pippa Small, Solange Azagury-Partridge, Balenciaga, Chloé
casual	Topshop, Oasis, Zara, Designers at Debenhams, Warehouse, Knickerbox, Dune, Gap **Accessories** Designers at Debenhams, Zara	Whistles, Karen Millen, Jigsaw, French Connection, Hobbs, Calvin Klein, Bodas, Nuala **Accessories** Whistles, Karen Millen, Furla, Coccinelle	Joseph, Ralph Lauren, Plein Sud, Chloé, Paul and Joe, Prada, Gucci, Brora, CXD, Helmut Lang **Accessories** Hogan, Tods, Prada
trendy	Oasis, Monsoon, Zara, Warehouse, Knickerbox, Gap, H & M **Accessories** Zara, Accessorize, Office, Dune	Whistles, Jigsaw, Karen Millen, French Connection, Coast, Reiss, Press & Bastyan **Accessories** Whistles, Jigsaw, Karen Millen, LK Bennett	Red Hot, Jean Paul Gaultier, Missoni, Dries van Noten, Melissa Odabash, Allegra Hicks, Ann Louise Roswald **Accessories** Stephane Kélian, Bottega Veneta, Erickson Beamon, J & M Davidson, Steinberg and Tolkien

work wear/the executive

	£	££	£££
smart	H & M, Warehouse, Zara, Oasis, Topshop, Aristoc, Marks & Spencer, Dorothy Perkins, Mango, Kookai **Accessories** Zara, Office, Oasis, Topshop, Aristoc, Freedom @ Topshop, Mikey, Accessorize	Karen Millen, Hobbs, Jigsaw, LK Bennett, Bella Freud for Jaeger, Reiss, Bodas, Calvin Klein Underwear **Accessories** Pied à Terre, Jigsaw, LK Bennett, Karen Millen, Whistles	Vanessa Bruno, Rozae Nichols, Prada, Chloé, Dosa, Diane von Furstenberg, Vivienne Westwood, Pringle, Wolford, Jasper Conran, DKNY, Nicole Farhi, Calvin Klein, Ralph Lauren, Armani, **Accessories** Pippa Small, Zilo, Solange Azagury-Partridge, Merola, Erickson Beamon,
casual	Designers at Debenhams, Oasis, Zara, Dorothy Perkins, H & M, Gap, Warehouse, Morgan, Kookai, Mango **Accessories** Office, Dune, Faith, H & M, Designers at Debenhams, Mango	Hobbs, Jigsaw, Whistles, French Connection, LK Bennett, Karen Millen, John Smedley **Accessories** Hobbs, Jigsaw, L K Bennett, Karen Millen	Ralph Lauren, Nicole Farhi, Joseph, Armani, Chloé, Prada, Calvin Klein, Temperley, Pringle, Gucci, Burberry, Chanel **Accessories** Stephane Kélian, Joseph, Hermès, Prada
trendy	Zara, Oasis, Designers at Debenhams, Monsoon, Warehouse, H & M, Dorothy Perkins, Principles, Dune, Marks & Spencer, Gap Body, Knickerbox **Accessories** Dune, Zara, Office	Jigsaw, Hobbs, Calvin Klein Underwear, Whistles, Karen Millen, Coast, Press & Bastyan **Accessories** Russell & Bromley, Jigsaw, Karen Millen, Whistles, Hobbs	Prada, Donna Karen, Marc Jacobs, Temperley, Louis Vuitton, Chloé, Ann Louise Roswald, Boyd, Megan Park, Rozae Nichols **Accessories** Prada, Sigerson Morrison, Marc Jacobs, Fenwick, Stephane Kélian

work wear/the pa

	£	££	£££
smart	Designer at Debenhams, H & M, Zara, Warehouse, Oasis, Dorothy Perkins, Principles, Mango, Monsoon **Accessories** Accessorize, Zara	Jigsaw, Hobbs, French Connection, Karen Millen, LK Bennett, Whistles, Reiss, John Smedley **Accessories** Jigsaw, Hobbs, Russell & Bromley, Whistles	Armani, Prada, Gucci, Dries van Noten, Vivienne Westwood, Ralph Lauren, Calvin Klein, Brora, Joseph, Alexander McQueen, Pringle, Nicole Farhi, CXD **Accessories** Stephane Kélian, Joseph, J & M Davidson
casual	Oasis, H & M, Mango, Gap, Marks & Spencer, Designers at Debenhams, Topshop, Dorothy Perkins **Accessories** Zara, Gap, Accessorize, Oasis, Topshop Office, Dune, Faith, Mango	Jigsaw, Whistles, Karen Millen, Miss Sixty, French Connection, Michael Stars, John Smedley **Accessories** Nike, Puma, Jigsaw, Whistles	Joseph, Seven, Marc by Marc Jacobs, Calvin Klein, Earl Jean, Joie, Nuala, Juicy Couture, Chloé, Ann Demeulemeester, Prada Sport **Accessories** Tods, Hogan, Nuala, Prada Sport
trendy	Topshop, Zara, H & M, Dorothy Perkins, Mango, Miss Selfridge, Pink Soda, Warehouse **Accessories** Freedom @ TopShop, Accessorize, Faith, Dune, Office	Day Birger et Mikkelsen, Jigsaw, Whistles, LK Bennett, French Connection, Nougat, Michael Stars, **Accessories** Agatha, Butler and Wilson,	Dries van Noten, Marc Jacobs, Miu Miu, Gharani Strok, Prada, Ralph Lauren, Temperley, Ann Louise Roswald, Luisa Beccaria, Marni, Rozae Nichols **Accessories** Zilo, Erickson Beamon, Pippa Small, Me and Ro @ Willma, Patch NYC @ Willma

tips

work wear

- **Learn to lay out a percentage of your wardrobe by outfits. Makes for stress-free getting ready in the morning – especially if you have thin or fat days**

- **Unless you work on a beauty counter, the workplace is not somewhere to ladle on the make-up – you know who you are**

- **If you work in an office with natural light, do your make-up in the same environment**

- **In case you need high heels for a meeting, keep a pair of simple pumps in your desk drawer to combine comfort with chic**

- **Personal smells can be very off-putting to co-workers and yet their embarrassment might prevent them from commenting. Check your underarm, feet and mouth with a good friend if you're getting dubious looks**

- **Have an emergency kit at work – spare stockings, clean knickers...**

work to play It's always the same. The one night you're going out is the same night your boss asks you to work late. You don't want to let him down, yet there's no way you're going to miss out on the party. You love your job, but not enough to sacrifice your personal life. You know that, but you want to keep your boss believing that you live to work. Keeping this lie alive without having to go to the party looking unwashed and in rags requires cunning planning and an ability to wave a magic wand. It's not a question of having a taxi waiting to whisk you home to a ready-drawn bath and laid-out clothes. That's way too stressful and far too expensive – a fantasy that only happens in fiction. Neither do you want to smuggle in a hanging bagful of glamour which then has to be left filled with the daytime tatters – and probably forgotten – in the party venue cloak-room. Clever transformations happen with the switch of a shoe and the swap of a top. Take heart, dear girls, you can have it all – a successful career and an exciting social life.

work
toplay

3

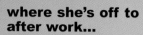

winter/day

✓ **where she's off to after work...**

a hot date at a smart dinner party

wants...

to look seductive to wow the hot date, but also maintain sophistication

winter/evening

✓ how to transform

Skirt stays, take off white vest to show revealing neckline

Remove coat and show some leg

Change sensible boots for strappy stilettos

Add glam jewellery and fishnets

what it says about you

'I know I'm very sexy but I decide who I'm available to. I am totally in control and any one-night stands or post-coital dumping will be implemented by me.'

winter/day

✓ **where she's off to after work...**

drinking with girlfriends – with the presence of some eligible males a possibility

wants...

to look flipping gorgeous – just in case the eligible males do show up – with the illusion that she's made no effort at all

winter/evening

✓ **how to transform**

Un-cuff the jeans

Add a fun sexy belt

Change the thick sweater for a more revealing, fitted jumper

Add some pointy stiletto ankle-boots

what it says about you

'I'm just one of the girls having fun with my friends, but the one that the boys want to flock to.'

winter/day

✓ **where she's off to after work...**

meeting boyfriend's parents for the first time

wants...

to look dressed up but slightly conservative and in something his mum can identify with

winter/evening

✓ **how to transform**

Remove jeans and replace with fishnets

Exchange pumps for stiletto sling-backs

Add an interesting necklace or other piece of jewellery

what it says about you

'I'm a financially independent, well-brought-up girl who only wants to be with your son because I love him. I'm glamorous and fashionable but not tarty, so I won't embarrass you.'

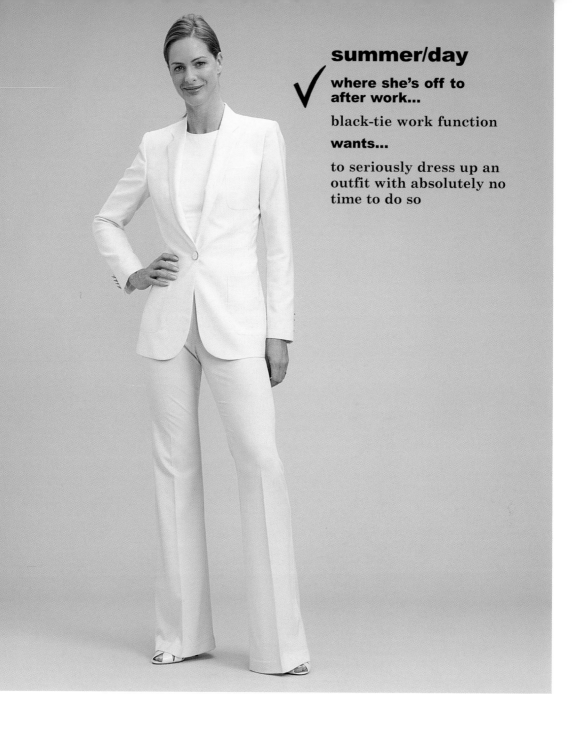

summer/day

✓ **where she's off to after work...**

black-tie work function

wants...

to seriously dress up an outfit with absolutely no time to do so

summer/evening

how to transform

Remove under-top

Put on choker or
opulent earrings

Change to gold
strappy high heels

Let your hair down

what it says about you

'I don't fuss too much with my clothes, I just look this good
naturally. I'm an individual with utterly impeccable taste,
but it's so innate I don't even notice.'

summer/day

✓ **where she's off to after work...**

an anniversary dinner with husband

wants...

to be dressed up and sexy for a very special night with the one I love

summer/evening

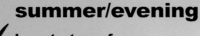

✓ **how to transform**

Swap trousers for long lacy green skirt

Change bra to one that emphasises cleavage and makes top look sexier

Add big antique earrings and tuck hair back to show them off

Take off knickers

what it says about you

'I'm your domestic goddess who manages to juggle my job, with kids, home and husband. My sexiness is for you and you alone.'

summer/day

✓ **where she's off to after work...**

a summer drinks party

wants...

to crank up the hip voltage in something that's individual and stands out in a crowd

work to play trendy

summer/evening

✓ **how to transform**

Switch flats for open-toed high heels

Add extra-long floppy trousers under the dress

Make sure jewels are extra distinctive

Put hair up

what it says about you

'I have a fascinating life. I'm the most interesting person at this party and you can't do better than to talk to me – if I let you.'

work to play/winter

	£	££	£££
smart	Gap Body, Knickerbox, Marks & Spencer, H & M, Zara, Designers at Debenhams, Dune, Morgan, Oasis, Mango, Warehouse, Monsoon, Topshop, Dorothy Perkins, Kookai **Accessories** Mikey, Accessorize, Zara, Dorothy Perkins, Freedom @ Topshop, Topshop, Office, Faith, Dune	Fantasie, Karen Millen, Wolford, Hobbs, Whistles, Press & Bastyan, French Connection, Bodas, Calvin Klein Underwear, LK Bennett, Reiss, Uth **Accessories** LK Bennett, Pied à Terre, Agatha, Butler and Wilson, Jigsaw, Kurt Geiger	Prada, Gucci, La Perla, Chloé, Temperley, Joseph, Vanessa Bruno, Rozae Nichols, Celine, Michael Kors, Chanel, Alexander McQueen, Givenchy, Boss Woman **Accessories** Pippa Small, Gina, Christian Louboutin, Stephane Kélian, Merola, Erickson Beamon, Jimmy Choo
casual	Zara, H & M, Gap, Topshop, Oasis, Warehouse **Accessories** Mikey, Freedom @ Topshop, Peekaboo @ Topshop, Zara	French Connection, Jigsaw, John Smedley, Whistles, Michael Stars, Nougat, Karen Millen, Reiss **Accessories** Pied à Terre, Russell and Bromley, Whistles, Butler and Wilson, Agatha	Marc Jacobs, Joie, Earl Jean, Juicy Couture, Chloé, Joseph, Ann Louise Roswald, Temperley, Seven **Accessories** Stephane Kélian, Joseph, Fenwick, Sigerson Morrison, J & M Davidson
trendy	Gap, Zara, Oasis, Warehouse, Designers at Debenhams, Principles, Mango, Kookai, Morgan, H & M **Accessories** Accessorize, Freedom @ Topshop, Mikey, Zara, Bertie, Faith, Office	French Connection, Whistles, LK Bennett, Reiss, Karen Millen, Press & Bastyan **Accessories** Butler and Wilson, Agatha, Pied à Terre, LK Bennett, Kurt Geiger	Diane Von Furstenberg, Seven, Joie, Juicy Couture, Joseph, Prada **Accessories** Joseph, Prada, Christian Louboutin, Sigerson Morrison, Gina, Jimmy Choo, Manolo Blahnik, Erickson Beamon, Merola, Pippa Small, Me and Ro

work to play/summer

	£	££	£££
smart	Zara, Warehouse, Oasis, Designers at Debenhams, Topshop, Knickerbox, Marks & Spencer, Gap Body, Dorothy Perkins, Principles **Accessories** Zara, Freedom @ Topshop, Mikey, Zara, Office, Dune, Faith, Bertie, Accessorize	Jigsaw, Karen Millen, Reiss, LK Bennett, Jaeger, Hobbs, Calvin Klein Underwear, Whistles **Accessories** Butler and Wilson, Pebble, Agatha, Pied à Terre, LK Bennett, Jigsaw, Post Mistress	Chloé, Paule Ka, Paul and Joe, Prada, Armani, Calvin Klein, La Perla, Vivienne Westwood **Accessories** Gina, Jimmy Choo, Sigerson Morrison Merola, Erickson Beamon, Solange Azagury-Partridge, Pippa Small
casual	Zara, H & M, Oasis, Warehouse, Gap Body, Monsoon, Pink Soda, Topshop, **Accessories** Faith, Office, Dune, Accessorize, Mikey, Topshop	Jigsaw, Whistles, Hobbs, Karen Millen, Reiss, French Connection, Frost French, Nougat **Accessories** Butler and Wilson, Agatha, Jigsaw, Whistles, LK Bennett, Pied à Terre, Post Mistress	Dosa, Chloé, Temperley, The West Village, Alberta Ferretti, Marni, Diane von Furstenberg, Dries van Noten, Etro, Boyd, Megan Park ,Rachel Robarts **Accessories** Erickson Beamon, Pippa Small, Solange Azagury-Partridge, Gina, Sigerson Morrison, Chloé
trendy	Zara, H & M, Oasis, Dorothy Perkins, Topshop, Miss Selfridge, Kookai, Mikey, Warehouse, Pink Soda, Peekaboo @ Topshop, Mossie @ Topshop **Accessories** Office, Dune, Bertie, Topshop, Accessorize	French Connection, Sara Berman, Jigsaw, Reiss, Whistles, Butler and Wilson, Agatha, Karen Millen, LK Bennett **Accessories** Butler and Wilson, Agatha, Whistles, Jigsaw, Pebble	Temperley, Chloé, Boyd, Missoni, Joseph, Megan Park, Alberta Ferretti, Donna Karan, Blumarine, Marc Jacobs, Louis Vuitton **Accessories** Pippa Small, Solange Azagury-Partridge, Zilo, Me and Ro, Christian Louboutin, Gina, Merola, Jimmy Choo, Sigerson Morrison

work to play

- Keep a make-up bag at work that also contains deodorant, toothpaste and cologne

- If you have time, it's better to re-do your make-up, especially if you've had a long day and feel tired

- In the summer have some talc and footspray at the office for refreshing sweaty feet at the end of a long day

- Keep a pair of great heels at the office – in the summer, silver or gold and in the winter, black stilettos

- Make sure you have a fresh pair of fishnets in your desk drawer so you can make a quick transformation for a last-minute invitation

- Take out cash at lunchtime – even if you're being taken on a date – so you're always independent

- Have a smaller evening bag handy to take out with you

- Keep vitamin C supplements (Berocca, Emergen-C) in your desk for a perk up before you go out

- If you suspect – or hope – it's going to be a long night and you might have to go straight to the office, have something fresh in your drawer to avoid office gossip

- If your hair is looking lank by the end of the day, slick it back if short, or put up in a ponytail if long

tips

school events There's something about school that makes you feel like a child again. It's the smell of discipline and detention that hangs in the air. Susannah finds herself automatically circumspect in front of her four-year-old son's teacher, even though the girl is a decade and a half younger. She will endeavour to look tidy and together as opposed to displaying the truth of a chaotic start to the day. As a hang-over from our own school days, we assume teachers to be disapproving, and as parents we imagine any slip-up from us will lead to the condemnation of our kids. As the children get older, our appearance becomes imperative for the sake of their relationships with friends. If mum looks cool it reflects fantastically on them. If you are aware of this, the pressure of what to wear at school events is high. Not only do you have to score points with the teaching staff, but you also have to win the approval of your children's friends. Turning up fresh from being dragged out of domestic may-hem will do neither you nor your kids any favours at all. Combining a nod to what's in fashion with respect for the institutional surroundings will keep everyone happy and your self-respect intact.

school events

4

sports day

✗ Shoe heels will continually sink into the ground

Jeans skirt inhibits movement

Top is so low-cut that any activity could cause tits to fly out and flash everyone

what it says about you

'I really care what the other mothers (and fathers) think of me and always want to be more trendy and cool than them. Sports day... what sports day?'

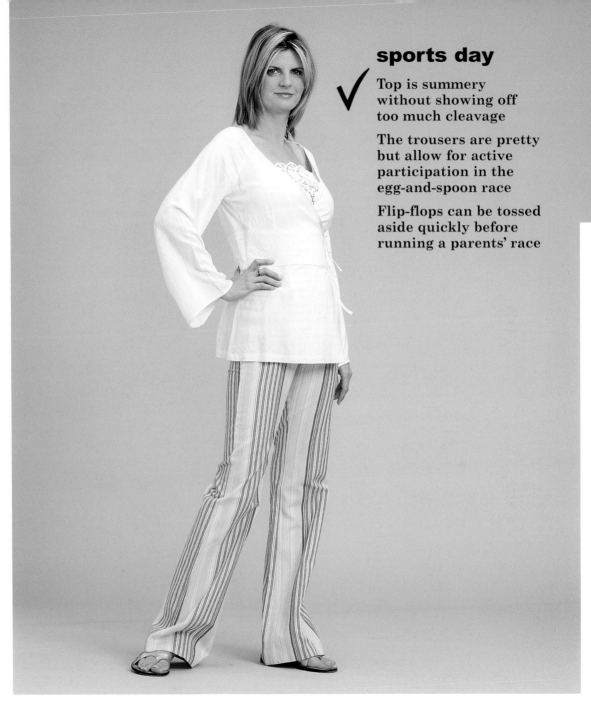

sports day

✓ Top is summery without showing off too much cleavage

The trousers are pretty but allow for active participation in the egg-and-spoon race

Flip-flops can be tossed aside quickly before running a parents' race

what it says about you

'I love sports day and I'll muck in and have a laugh. My kids are my focus today but I love to have a natter with the other parents.'

school play

✗ Wrap shawls are very headmistressy

Looks like you're about to leave at any moment

The suit and tied-back hair look too stern for a young mum

what it says about you

'My children eat all their greens, say please and thank you, open doors and do their homework on time. They'll go to university and become prime minister.'

school play

✓ Similar colours streamline separates

A great coat can change a running around daytime outfit into something more special

Hair down looks more relaxed and less severe

what it says about you

'I am a responsible mother who's sensitive to blending into the audience. I may have a high-powered career but I still make time to look good for my kids.'

pta meeting

X The jeans are messy and dirty looking

The layered untucked tops suggest a tardy, disorganised mother

Sunglasses on the head remind the teacher of a school rebel who hasn't grown up

Battered shoes look scruffy

what it says about you

'I don't really have time for this because I've got to run to the supermarket. Chaos is the key word for my family's lifestyle. What you tell me will go in one ear and out the other.'

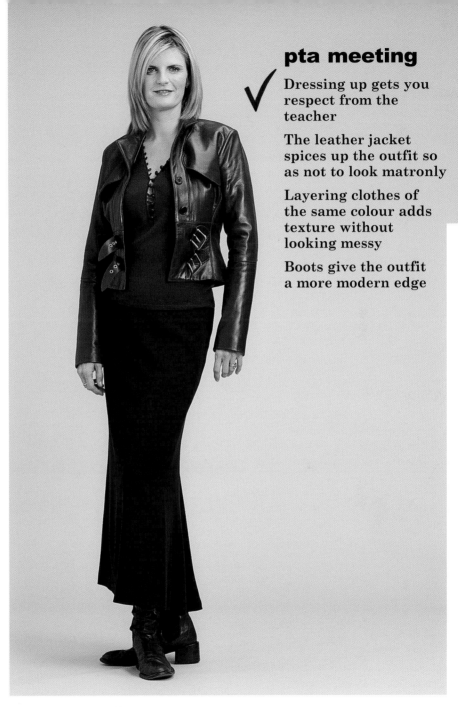

pta meeting

✓ Dressing up gets you respect from the teacher

The leather jacket spices up the outfit so as not to look matronly

Layering clothes of the same colour adds texture without looking messy

Boots give the outfit a more modern edge

what it says about you

'I respect the school. I'm a responsible mother who deserves to have children. I'm young at heart and have enormous fun with my kids. I want the best for them at school and expect you, Miss, to provide that.'

carol concert

Red and black bring out the tart in everyone – NOT festive

The combo of a high slit, fishnets and ankle booties smack of trying too hard to be young and sexy

Bright red lipstick is too flashy for the occasion

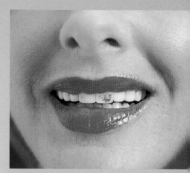

what it says about you

'I am slutty, available and a bad role model for my children. I flirt with all my teenage son's friends – mmm, I think I need a chat with that maths master.'

carol concert

✓ **Subtle sparkle is a merry nod to the festive season**

Dark colours allow your child, not you, to shine

Boots tone down the effect of the sequins

what it says about you

'I'm a desirable Yummy Mummy and my child's friends will always be welcome and have fun when they come to play at our house.'

school events

	£	££	£££
sports day	H & M, Mango, Zara, Warehouse, Marks & Spencer, George @ Asda, Florence and Fred @ Tesco, Dorothy Perkins, Principles, La Redoute, Boden, Gap Body, Knickerbox **Accessories** Accessorize, Office, Bertie, Ravel, H & M, Zara, Faith, Dune	French Connection, Michael Stars, Whistles, Sweaty Betty, Frankie B, Urban Outfitters, Calvin Klein Underwear **Accessories** Birkenstock, Nike, Puma, Russell & Bromley	Dosa, Marni, Joseph, Dolce and Gabbana, Prada Sport, Polo Ralph Lauren, Melissa Odabash, Juicy Couture, Earl Jean, Seven, Nuala, Paul and Joe **Accessories** Sigerson Morrison, Tods, Nuala, Prada Sport, Hogan
school play	Zara, Warehouse, Mango, H & M, Designers at Debenhams, Accessorize, Mikey, Freedom @ Topshop, Oasis, Dorothy Perkins **Accessories** Freedom @ Topshop, Oasis, Zara, H & M, River Island, Gap, Nine West, Faith	Jigsaw, French Connection, Karen Millen, Press & Bastyan, Michael Stars, John Smedley, LK Bennett, Hobbs, Whistles **Accessories** LK Bennett, Hobbs, Whistles, Jigsaw, Karen Millen, Kurt Geiger	Boyd, Temperley, Ronit Zilkha, Prada, Chloé, Joseph, J & M Davidson, Brora, CXD **Accessories** Prada, Chloé, Stephane Kélian, Jimmy Choo, Christian Louboutin, Joseph, J & M Davidson
pta meeting	Monsoon, Zara, H & M, Designers at Debenhams, Oasis, Warehouse, Topshop, Mango **Accessories** Office, Bertie, Nine West, Jones the Bootmaker, Nine West, Accessorize	Jigsaw, French Connection, Hobbs, Whistles, Michael Stars, John Smedley, Karen Millen, Coast **Accessories** Hobbs, Whistles, Kurt Geiger, LK Bennett, Karen Millen, Jigsaw	Joseph, Gucci, Prada, Alexander McQueen, Chloé, Dries van Noten, Brora, Pringle, Marilyn Moore, Vivienne Westwood, Vanessa Bruno, Rozae Nichols **Accessories** Prada, Gucci, Sigerson Morrison
carol concert	Zara, Designers at Debenhams, Oasis, Warehouse, H & M, Mango, Topshop **Accessories** Bertie, Nine West, Topshop, Faith, Office, Zara	French Connection, Karen Millen, Jigsaw, Press & Bastyan, John Smedley, Hobbs **Accessories** Russell & Bromley, LK Bennett, Jigsaw, Karen Millen	Nicole Farhi, Plein Sud, Temperley, Ralph Lauren, Prada, Alexander McQueen, Chloé, Stephane Kelian, Boss Woman, Armani, Gucci **Accessories** Stephane Kélian, Prada

school events

- Remember you're no longer at school – so enjoy yourself

- Look clean and tidy but don't overdress or look overtly sexy

- Keep make-up subtle

- If you're not a parent there are fewer constraints about how eccentric you can look

- Don't overdo the sucking up to teachers. They will only smell a rat

- Too much boasting about your child alienates other parents

- Keep camera paraphernalia to a minimum

- If you have teenagers, don't try to chat too much to their friends and compete with their put-on coolness. You'll only embarrass your own child

summer wedding Ah, the joys of a summer wedding. Balmy air dotted with mayflies; the gentle evening light softening out the skin tone as effectively as Botox; barefoot bridesmaids, glowing from the warm afternoon sun, fluttering around the wedding cake. You cast your eye fondly across the idyllic scene when, all of a sudden, hell arrives in clumpy black shoes and a crochet shawl. It was too perfect to be true and there's always one guest who lands like a sick joke, fresh from the planet of Bad Taste. The unknown being is confused about the seasons. She knows not if it is summer or winter. Her time clock, too, has gone awry. Is it day or night? Eradicating any chance of catching a chill, breaking out into a sweat or getting caught out by her period, she wears thick flesh-coloured tights bulging over wide-strapped black sandals. Her 'handy' shawl is easy to discard after a strenuous bop around her holdall which hides a cash-and-carry sized pack of panty liners. She has thought of everything – and it shows in her outfit. She doesn't look chic. She is a one-woman band of fashion blunders. Do you know this woman? If so read on.

summer wedding

5

day

✗ Everything is matching even the bag and hat

Jacket length is dated and disproportionate on any body shape

The entire outfit shows any lack of individuality

If it's sunny, the fabric will be suffocating

what it says about you

'I have no imagination, but I don't need one because all that matters is that I fit in with all the other middle-aged prudes. You know I've worn this suit many times before – it's my wedding suit.'

day

A floaty summer dress that flatters the body shape is the most elegant attire for a daytime summer wedding

Look is unfussy yet feminine

Hat picks out the palest colour in the dress, not the darkest

Accessories stand out for the key pieces they are

what it says about you

'I don't want to outshine the bride or her mother. I appreciate what a special day it is and have gone the extra mile with my look.'

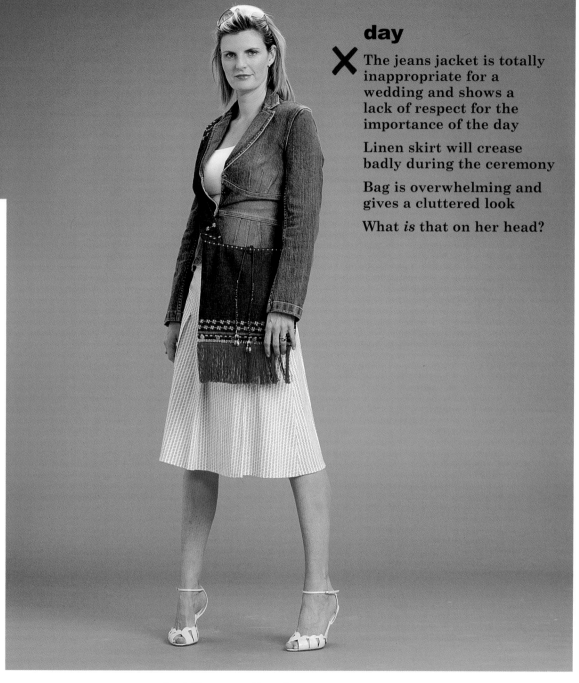

day

✗ The jeans jacket is totally inappropriate for a wedding and shows a lack of respect for the importance of the day

Linen skirt will crease badly during the ceremony

Bag is overwhelming and gives a cluttered look

What *is* that on her head?

what it says about you

'I don't care that I'm still on the shelf and I don't like weddings so don't want to make any effort. In fact, I'm too cool to conform to tradition.'

day

✓ Mixing patterns works well when the fabrics and colours are similar

Hat is a fun talking piece but not over-bearing

Shoes are sexy but give enough support for walking so you don't look a complete dork

what it says about you

'I'm going to have a ball. I'm fantastic fun to hang with and I'll drink you under the table but still be together enough to catch the bride's bouquet.'

evening

✗ The tweed jacket is behind the times and too uncomfortable to dance in

Black accessories are too strong a contrast with the pastel colours

The choker labels the wearer

what it says about you

'OK, ya. Once I've got you, you won't escape. I'll bang on for Britain about fascinating subjects such as the weather, my Jack Russell and how I've known the bride since she was that high.'

evening

✓ The clothing could be vintage but it's from a High Street shop

The colours of the outfit echo those in the hairpiece and so bring harmony

A sexy dress to dance in

Slinky cardigan and fab evening bag complete a stunning look

what it says about you

'I understand the sobriety of a religious ceremony, but I fully intend on letting my hair down later when the dancing starts.'

evening

✗ Navy and red never look good together unless another colour is involved

The flowers would look better if they were just in the hair

Crochet cardigans look tired and frumpy wherever they are from

what it says about you

'I need frivolous clothes to compensate for my lack of personality. I'll be hard work to talk to until a couple of bottles have slipped down my throat. Then I'll embarrass myself on the dance floor before rushing off to vomit in the ice bucket.'

evening

✓ Faux mink jacket adds a touch of glamour and covers up bigger arms more elegantly than a shawl

No hat means no flat hair underneath

Sequin detail means that the shorter length still looks formal enough

what it says about you

'I'll be more than happy to let you peer down my cleavage just so long as you keep your hands to yourself. Once you've met me you won't want to leave my side.'

summer wedding/day

smart	£	££	£££
	Zara, Oasis, Warehouse, Designers at Debenhams, Kookai, Monsoon	Karen Millen, Whistles, Press & Bastyan, Reiss, Miliana T @ The Cross, Jigsaw, Bella Freud for Jaeger	Prada, Alberta Ferretti, Temperley, Paul Smith, Chanel, Betty Jackson, Elspeth Gibson, Diane von Furstenberg, Ronit Zilkha
	Accessories Office, Dune, Faith, Mikey, Freedom @ Topshop, Bertie, Accessorize	**Accessories** LK Bennett, Kurt Geiger, Butler and Wilson, Agatha, Jigsaw, Pied à Terre, Coccinelle	**Accessories** Gina, Jimmy Choo, Manolo Blahnik, Christian Louboutin, Sigerson Morrison, Paul Smith, Philip Treacy, Jamin Puech, Erickson Beamon, Zilo, Solange Azagury-Partridge,

trendy	£	££	£££
	Kal Kaur Rai, Pink Soda, Zara, Warehouse, Office, Oasis, Accessorize, Mikey, Topshop, Peekaboo @ Topshop, Dune, Portobello Market	Karen Millen, Whistles, Reiss, Miliana T @ The Cross, French Connection, Jigsaw	Temperley, Boyd, Megan Park, Jamin Puech, Gharani Strok, Paul Smith, Luisa Beccaria, Shirin Guild, Moschino, Virginia, Steinberg and Tolkien
	Accessories Office, Accessorize, Mikey, Freedom @ Topshop, Peekaboo @ Topshop, Dune, Portobello Market	**Accessories** Whistles, LK Bennett, Free Lance, Pied à Terre, Kurt Geiger, Jigsaw	**Accessories** Gabriella Ligenza, Philip Treacy, Christian Louboutin Jamin Puech, Manolo Blahnik, Paul Smith, Virginia, Steinberg and Tolkien

summer wedding/night

smart	£	££	£££
	Monsoon, Zara, Accessorize, Oasis, Designers at Debenhams, Warehouse, Principles, Dorothy Perkins, Kal Kaur Rai @ Topshop, Pink Soda,	Karen Millen, Press and Bastyan, Whistles Reiss, Jigsaw, French Connection,	Ben di Lisi, Valentino, Prada, Celine, Armani, Christian Dior, YSL, Alberta Ferretti, Betty Jackson
	Accessories Zara, Accessorize, Freedom @ Topshop, Mikey	**Accessories** Butler and Wilson, Agatha, Pied à Terre, LK Bennett, Kurt Geiger, Jigsaw	**Accessories** Judith Leiber, Swarovski, Philip Treacy, Erickson Beamon, Pippa Small, Merola, Basia Zarzycka, Jimmy Choo

trendy	£	££	£££
	Zara, Oasis, Designers at Debenhams, Betty Jackson at Freemans, Kookai, Warehouse, Portobello Market, Peekaboo @ Topshop	French Connection, Reiss, Whistles, LK Bennett, Butler and Wilson, Jigsaw, Karen Millen	Ungaro, Gharani Strok, Temperley, Betty Jackson, Elspeth Gibson, Luisa Beccaria, Gina, Boyd, Basia Zarzycka, Megan Park, Chloé, Virginia, Moschino
	Accessories Accessorize, Mikey, Freedom @ Topshop	**Accessories** LK Bennett, Butler and Wilson, Kurt Geiger, Jigsaw, Pied à Terre, Agatha, Karen Millen	**Accessories** Jimmy Choo, Gabriella Ligenza, Gina, Basia Zarzycka, Philip Treacy, Jamin Puech, Virginia, Steinberg and Tolkien

summer wedding

- Never outshine the bride unless she's marrying your ex-lover

- If you don't know how to deal with an ex or unwanted attention, wear a wide-brimmed hat to avoid too much physical contact

- Don't wear white at a conventional wedding

- If the reception is anywhere near a lawn, don't wear a thin heel

- Don't use a big bag

- Trousers are fine – as long as they're not the ones you might wear to the office

- If the wedding is in daylight, do your make-up in daylight

- Get a pedicure if you are wearing open-toed sandals and pay special attention to your heels

- A fan can keep you cool in church and act as a flirtatious accessory

- If you have a small forehead, wear a hat with a tall crown to balance out your head

- If it's wet, don't wear open-toed sandals or suede shoes

tips

winter wedding Phlumph! Wedding invitation lands on door mat. 'Oh, so and so is getting married. Must get my suit out. Better get my coat dry-cleaned as it's bound to be cold. Thank goodness I bought that hat for Jane's wedding in the summer. It will go perfectly with my bag and shoe set.' Do we feel a uniform appearing? For some reason winter weddings are more inclined to bring out the chain-store manageress in women. Sensible suits are much in evidence, often coupled with a heavy winter coat and a navy or black hat that bears no relation to the rest of the outfit. Colour is often abandoned in the colder months, leaving a ceremony more in tune with that for a passing relative. One guest might break the drab ranks, but rest assured she'll do so in bottle green or maroon. If there's an evening do, then style spirals into strappy dresses compromised by something warm, as inappropriate as the presence of the groom's ex-wife. While this is, of course, a wild generalisation, many of you will secretly recognise elements of the Archetypal Winter Wedding Attire. Relieve yourself from the chains of mediocrity by being an outstandingly stunning guest.

winter wedding

6

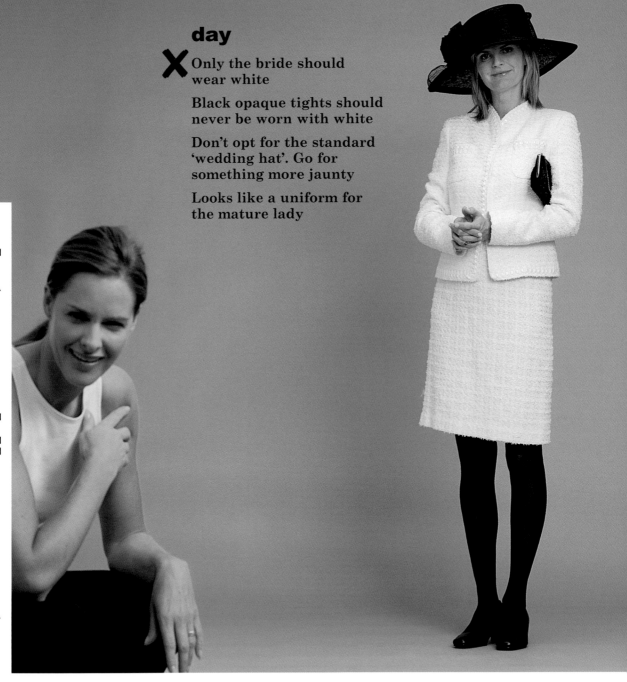

✗ Only the bride should wear white

Black opaque tights should never be worn with white

Don't opt for the standard 'wedding hat'. Go for something more jaunty

Looks like a uniform for the mature lady

winter wedding smart

what it says about you

'I feel safe in the pigeonhole of middle age. It's not often that I dress up because I don't get out much these days.'

day

✓ A frock coat can keep you warm and looking chic at the same time

The coat can be worn for everyday occasions as well

Elegant, flat leather boots help you navigate any dirty country lanes

A sharp hat is best shown off with simple tailoring

what it says about you

'Oh, this is something I threw on at the last minute. But I can bring it together because I understand the importance of good tailoring.'

day

✗ Looking trendy is not about wearing work clothes to a wedding

A suede skirt and suede jacket should never be worn together – whether they match or not

Even if you don't wear a hat you should still look as though you've made an effort

what it says about you

'This suit is so useful that I've worn it to death. I have no sense of occasion and know my friends love me anyway for my personality.'

day

✓ Fur gives the wearer instant glamour

Burgundy and turquoise can look great together

Separates are more interesting than a suit

A combination of fabrics gives an opulent look

what it says about you

'My life is too full to have the time to buy a special wedding outfit. And it's not necessary because I'm versatile by nature. I can fit in anywhere and love talking to anyone so I'm the ideal wedding guest.'

evening

✗ A huge coat overpowers what's underneath and takes all the elegance out of an outfit

Open-toed sandals look wrong with the coat (and your feet will freeze)

All black is safe – but very uninspiring

winter wedding smart

what it says about you

'I'm a very creative person, with a passion for cats and street art. My star sign is Virgo with Aries rising and I have a colonic once a month.'

evening

✓ A fitted jacket and long skirt flatter most figures and give a long lean silhouette

Wearing a printed skirt and a darker jacket is good if you are bigger up top (try the reverse if you are bigger down below)

Later, the jacket can be removed to show off a black-tie outfit

what it says about you

'I respect the seriousness of the marriage vows; yet I intend to let my hair down at the party without disturbing my outfit. If you're lucky I'll whip off my jacket to reveal a little more.'

evening

✗ Black cheapens the vibrancy of the skirt.

Fur hat is too daytime

An ankle-skimming skirt looks the wrong length with kitten-heeled boots

what it says about you

'My hat is from Prada, the jacket McQueen, the skirt Missoni, boots by Stephane Kélian. I love YSL and think Tom Ford is a genius... I'm not boring you am I?'

evening

✓ This demonstrates how mixing designer, vintage and High Street works well

Mixing patterns succeeds when the same colours are used

A long skirt looks great with high heels that cannot be seen

what it says about you

'Fashion is my passion, but I keep my clothing sources to myself. You certainly won't be bored by me at dinner and if you're stuck for something to say, tell me you adore my butterflies.'

winter wedding/day

	£	££	£££
smart	Zara, Oasis, H & M, Mango, Marks & Spencer, Designers at Debenhams, Monsoon, Kookai, Principles, Dorothy Perkins **Accessories** Accessorize, Topshop, Designers at Debenhams, Office, Dune, Faith	Jigsaw, Karen Millen, Whistles, Reiss, Uth, Jaeger, LK Bennett, Fred Bare, Hobbs, John Smedley, Press & Bastyan **Accessories** Jigsaw, Karen Millen, Whistles, Hobbs, LK Bennett, Fred Bare, Kurt Geiger	Chloé, Prada, Missoni, Karl Donoghue, Joseph, Ann Louise Roswald, Temperley, Boyd, Alberta Ferretti, Marilyn Moore, Vivienne Westwood **Accessories** Karl Donoghue, Joseph, Philip Treacy, Stephane Kélian, Christian Louboutin, Scorah Patullo
trendy	Zara, Designers at Debenhams, Oasis, Hennes, Warehouse, Mango, Monsoon **Accessories** Faith, Dune, Office, Designers at Debenhams, Zara	French Connection, Hobbs, LK Bennett, Reiss, Jigsaw, Karen Millen, Coast, Press & Bastyan, John Smedley **Accessories** Hobbs, LK Bennett, Jigsaw, Karen Millen	Temperley, Alberta Feretti, Boyd, Gabriella Ligenza, Megan Park, Jimmy Choo, Stephane Kélian, Sigerson Morrison, Joseph, Virginia **Accessories** Gabriella Ligenza, Jimmy Choo, Stephane Kélian, Sigerson Morrison, Joseph, Virginia

winter wedding/evening

	£	££	£££
smart	Zara, Oasis, H & M, Marks & Spencer, Gap Body, Kookai, Principles, Designers at Debenahams, Pink Soda, Topshop, Warehouse, Monsoon, Dorothy Perkins, Wallis **Accessories** Office, Faith, Dune, Freedom @Topshop, Accessorize, Zara	Jigsaw, Karen Millen, Reiss, LK Bennett, French Connection, Nougat, Press & Bastyan **Accessories** Butler and Wilson, Agatha, LK Bennett, Pied à Terre	Dries van Noten, Etro, Elspeth Gibson, Chloé, Vivienne Westwood, Armani, YSL, Temperley, Ungaro, Alberta Ferretti, Escada, Ben di Lisi, Basia Zarzycka **Accessories** Gina, Jimmy Choo, Erickson Beamon, Merola, Christian Louboutin, Basia Zarzycka
trendy	Monsoon, Zara, Warehouse, Designers at Debenhams, Office, Faith, Dune, Monsoon, Dorothy Perkins, Wallis, Oasis, Freedom @ Topshop, Peekaboo @ Topshop, Portobello Market, Mikey **Accessories** Designers at Debenhams, Office, Faith, Dune, Freedom @ Topshop, Peekaboo @ Topshop, Portobello Market, Mikey, Claire's Accessories, Accessorize	Jigsaw, Karen Millen, French Connection, Reiss, Whistles, Press & Bastyan, Nougat **Accessories** Jigsaw, Karen Millen, Pied à Terre, Whistles, Kurt Geiger	Etro, Chloé, Missoni, Alberta Ferretti, Boyd, Megan Park, Luisa Beccaria, Gabriella Ligenza, Ungaro, Basia Zarzycka, Ronit Zilkha **Accessories** Gabriella Ligenza, Phllip Treacy, Basia Zarzycka, Merola, Erickson Beamon

winter wedding

- Combine colours as nature intended. Think of the colours of leaves in autumn. Nothing jars

- Don't wear black to a wedding

- If it's really cold, consider wearing thermals underneath your outfit instead of a heavy coat that will only hide all the effort you've made

- Remember gloves keep you warm and add an element of elegance – as long as they are not black and woolly

- Check that the shadow from your hat does not accentuate the dark circles under your eyes

- Don't wear a summer hat with a winter outfit

- Blusher is even more important in winter, especially if you suffer from a sallow complexion

- Even if it's a Christmassy wedding, don't go over-the-top glitzy on the make-up

- If tights are involved in an outfit and you're in a potentially splintery church, carry a spare pair

tips

summer holiday The thought of having to step into a bikini fills all but the mad with a fit of panic. The thought of our pallid bodies emerging on the beach as radiating beacons of mottled skin, further defaced by cellulite-infested thighs is enough to send us into eternal seclusion. Tabloids expound miracle 'Bikini Diets' and magazines tell us how to achieve a polished bronze hide, the underlying message being that your body has to be marble hard, size Stupidly Thin and golden brown before venturing anywhere near the ghastly swimsuit. Oh please. What crap. No wonder we all feel such trepidation before stripping off in public. But there are ways and means to cover bad bits in a nonchalant fashion, just as there are fabulous beach looks that detract any onlookers from your lack of tan and tone. In a weird way people are far more likely to notice a disgusting swimsuit than they are a saggy arse. Once the sun goes down it's easy to look carefree and informally stylish. This can be achieved with old friends you've had in your closet for years – just be sure they aren't frumpy, dated or too over the top. Have a good one and don't forget to send us a postcard!

summer
holiday

7

on the beach

✗ Diamonds with swim-suits are a figment of Jackie Collins' imagination

Although black can be slimming, when teamed with gold sandals and jewellery it's too Palm Beach

Too much make-up will only run when the sun gets hot

what it says about you

'I killed off all five of my previous husbands and was wondering if you were rich enough to be the next? My beauty is only as thick as my make-up.'

on the beach

✓ A coordinated sarong and swimsuit works if the print is small and unobtrusive

Uniformity of pattern and colour is slimming and elongates the body

Flat gold sandals are glamorous without looking tarty

what it says about you

'I'm discreet and don't like attracting attention, but I'll be warm and friendly if you want to chat to me.'

on the beach

X

High-waisted, gathered shorts flatter no tummies

Shorts are best with a bikini top

Practical sandals look as if they're for the orthopaedically impaired

Trust us when we say her bum looks vast in these shorts

what it says about you

'I don't travel very well. My stomach can't take foreign muck so I take my bacon sarnies to the beach in tidy little Tupperware boxes.'

on the beach

✓ Low-waisted, flat-fronted longer shorts are the most flattering shape to wear. Team with a bikini top

Slip-on trainers are comfortable and flattering to the foot

Straw hat is simple but effective

what it says about you

'You'll have no idea whether I'm stinking rich or a pauper. I could own the most beautiful villa on the island or be sleeping under canvas on a camping site. You won't care either way cos I'm fab.'

on the beach

✗ Wearing everything from one label only accentuates a lack of taste

The bikini on its own would work with some contrasting accessories

Leave scarves to Greek widows or girls in their teens and twenties

what it says about you

'I think designer labels make me more interesting as a person. The truth is that I have no personality but since I'm easy meat after a few Tia Maria's, who cares?'

on the beach

A simple swimsuit covered by an exotic wrap makes a statement while covering parts of the body that you'd rather weren't seen when you come out of the water

Looks good and makes a security blanket for those with cellulite and pale skin

what it says about you

'I can't be arsed with all those pressurising bikini diets in the tabloids. I just cover up my dodgy bits with something fabulously ethnic.'

after sun

✗ Black for a summer evening can look too heavy

...especially when teamed with black leather shoes

Polyester fabrics make you sweat like pork in plastic

what it says about you

'I'm just like every other doughnut tourist, meaning I refuse to be adventurous and won't stray from the main drag of fast food outlets and tacky tourist shops.'

after sun

✓ Dress is shapely but has no tight waistband to dig into the flesh and exacerbate the pain of sunburnt skin

Gold sandals go with every summer evening outfit

Pale colours make the most of even the faintest tan

what it says about you

'Stand next to me to keep cool. My holiday has wound me down to the point where I can truly enjoy the bliss of taking time out.'

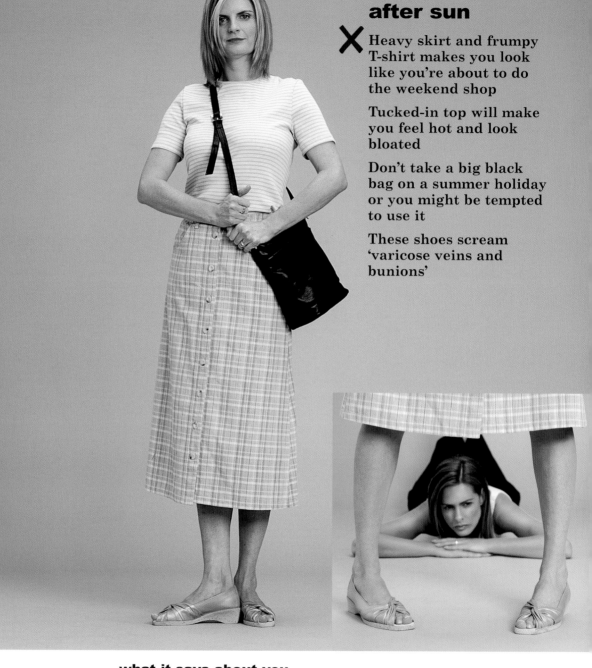

after sun

✗ Heavy skirt and frumpy T-shirt makes you look like you're about to do the weekend shop

Tucked-in top will make you feel hot and look bloated

Don't take a big black bag on a summer holiday or you might be tempted to use it

These shoes scream 'varicose veins and bunions'

what it says about you

'This is my first time abroad and as I'm such a novice traveller, my bag and I are open to every mugger and pickpocket on the Costa.'

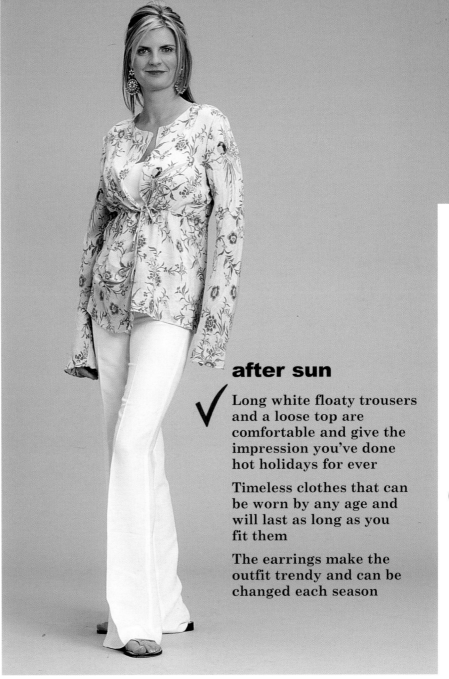

after sun

✓ Long white floaty trousers and a loose top are comfortable and give the impression you've done hot holidays for ever

Timeless clothes that can be worn by any age and will last as long as you fit them

The earrings make the outfit trendy and can be changed each season

what it says about you

'Where am I staying? Oh no, I live here. And if I really take to you, I'll tell you about this wonderful little bar where all the locals go.'

after sun

X Too much make-up on a tanned face makes it look dirty

Very high heels can make ankles and feet swell even more in the heat

Manmade fabrics turn skin into a swampy breeding ground for body odour

what it says about you

'Micro-minis are very 'in', which is great cos I can show off my mahogany tan. Getting a tan is all I really care about and I'm prepared to go to any lengths in self-humiliation to show it off.'

after sun

✓ **Silk is the coolest fabric to wear after a long day of sun**

Pale colours take the red out of sunburnt skin

A long skirt covers up pale legs if the tan hasn't set in

Flat sandals look good with a long skirt

It only takes one signature piece of clothing to look cool

what it says about you

'I don't need to roast myself on the beach. I'm just naturally golden all the year round and so cool.'

summer holiday/on the beach

	£	££	£££
smart	Zara, Topshop, Miss Selfridge, Monsoon, Next, Marks & Spencer, Warehouse, H & M **Accessories** Zara, Bertie, Office, Accessorize, Freedom @ Topshop, Claire's Accessories, Jasper Conran for Debenhams	Jigsaw, Whistles, Seafolly, Saltwater, French Connection, Cacharel, Miu Miu, Sportmax, Footprints **Accessories** LK Bennett, Cacharel, Jigsaw, Miu Miu	Prada, La Perla, Heidi Klein, Melissa Odabash, Allegra Hicks, Missoni, Versace, Celine, Pucci, Liza Bruce, Escada Sport, Armani **Accessories** Gina, Sigerson Morrison, Pucci, Gucci,
casual	H & M, Topshop, Next, Benetton, Adidas, Boden, Marks & Spencer, Gap **Accessories** Boden, Dune, Gap, Scholl, Office, Faith, Freedom @ Topshop, Accessorize	Birkenstock, Sweaty Betty, Seafolly, Diesel, Naf Naf, French Connection, Mambo, Nike, Puma **Accessories** Nike, Puma, Birkenstock,	Missoni, Marni, Juicy, Maharishi, Melissa Odabash, Prada Sport **Accessories** Anya Hindmarch, Nuala, Hogan, Orla Kiely, Kate Spade, Tods
trendy	H & M, Topshop, Next, Warehouse, Designers at Debenhams, Faith, Marks & Spencer, Dune, H & M, Miss Selfridge, New Look, Gap **Accessories** H & M, Freedom @ Topshop, Designers at Debenhams, Johnny Loves Rosie, Faith, Dune, Accessorize, Miss Selfridge, New Look, Ollie and Nic	Saltwater, The Jacksons, Whistles, Princess Tam Tam, Paule Ka, Paul and Joe, French Connection, Amanda+ Odi, Cacharel **Accessories** Inside Out, Ollie and Nic, French Connection, The Jacksons, Whistles	Anya Hindmarch, Sybil Stanislaus @ Ajanta, Melissa Odabash, Missoni, Pucci, Heidi Klein, Chloé, Gharani Strok, Allegra Hicks, Liza Bruce, Lara Bohnic, Louis Vuitton, Damaris, Juicy Couture, Betty Jackson, Ann Louise Roswald, Rachel Robarts, Coco De Mer **Accessories** Jade Jagger, Silhouette, Anya Hindmarch, Pippa Small, Orla Kiely

summer holiday/after sun

	£	££	£££
smart	Monsoon, Zara, H & M, Principles, Warehouse, Oasis, Designers at Debenhams **Accessories** Zara, H & M, Dune, Faith, Office, Mikey, Accessorize, Designers at Debenhams	Whistles, French Connection, Karen Millen, Autograph @ Marks and Spencer **Accessories** Whistles, Karen Millen, LK Bennett, Kurt Geiger, Kate Kuba, Pied à Terre,	Joseph, Temperley, Missoni, Alberta Ferretti, Celine, Prada, Escada **Accessories** Jimmy Choo, Manolo Blahnik, Gina, Sigerson Morrison, Jamin Puech
casual	Gap, H & M, Accessorize, Oasis, Warehouse, Zara, Principles, Designers at Debenhams, Topshop, New Look, East, Dorothy Perkins **Accessories** Dune, Office, Mikey, Freedom @ Topshop, East	Whistles, French Connection, Karen Millen, Jigsaw, Autograph @ Marks & Spencer **Accessories** L K Bennett, Pebble, Butler and Wilson	Ann Louise Roswald, Marni, Melissa Odabash, Tashia, Allegra Hicks, Rachel Robarts, Liza Bruce, Vanessa Bruno, Rozae Nichols, Kenzo, The West Village, **Accessories** Anya Hindmarch, Pippa Small, Me and Ro, Erickson Beaumon,
trendy	Zara, H & M, Oasis, Warehouse, Pink Soda, Designers at Debenhams, Kal Kaur Rai, Peekaboo @ Topshop, Portobello Market **Accessories** Dune, Office, Faith Freedom @ Topshop, Accessorise, Mikey	French Connection, Miliana T, Karen Millen, Jigsaw, Coast, Whistles, Cacharel **Accessories** Pebble, Lola Rose, Jigsaw, LK Bennett, Russell & Bromley	Temperley, Missoni, Miu Miu, Gharani Strok, Boyd, Pucci, Roberto Cavalli, Celine, Marni, Liza Bruce, Sybil Stanislaus **Accessories** Christian Louboutin, Gina, J Maskrey, Sigerson Morrison, Chloé, Me and Ro, Pippa Small, Erikson Beamon

summer holiday

- Make an effort to get your eyelashes tinted so you can avoid the panda look when you're in the water

- If you get your hair coloured, do it at least a week before to avoid drastic over-lifting by sun, sea and chlorine

- If you're going to have a fake tan, get it applied a couple of days before so if you wake up to a streaky situation you have time to remove it. St Tropez do an excellent remover

- Get waxing done at least a couple of days before so your skin has time to calm down

- Don't forget to wax your toes if you're a hairy girl (like Trinny) and belly button (if you're dark haired and it travels)

- If you're a sun worshipper, have a good old exfoliation before you go to remove any dead skin cell barriers to a gorgeous even tan

- If you tend to burn, don't pack any red or pink as they will only show up your lack of expertise with the SPFs

- Decant favoured luxury items into small plastic containers so you can fit even more beauty products into your suitcase. Check out Space NK, Muji and Boots for great containers, and Dyno at Rymans for marking them

- Add mosquito repellent to your aftersun so you never forget to apply some when there's a possibility of being bitten.

- When you get home, make a list of everything you didn't wear and don't take them next time if the climate and social situation are the same

tips

winter holiday Those of you who ski year in, year out will no doubt have got the vexed question what to wear both on and off the slopes down to a fine art. Instead of travelling with 35 suitcases, you limit your baggage to one neat holdall and a piece of hand luggage. You will know how to dress according to your downhill handicap. You won't be fooled by a beginner who's trussed up like Frans Klammer because the combination of professional clothing and quivering snow plough makes her look ridiculous as opposed to well... a beginner. If, though, you're a novice to the game you will quickly discover that gathering together a ski kit must be organised with scientific precision. It's no good just packing a load of heavy woollen goods and chucking in your favourite little black dress. You have to consider the freezing temperatures, hazardous walking conditions and how much cleavage the ski-club can take. You must take into account your skill – or lack of it – as a skier. When you're starting out, you may spend more time on the ground than on your skis, so a double-glazed ski-suit that keeps the snow from sneaking in when you fall can be a godsend.

winter
holiday

8

on the slopes/
professional

✗ Tight salopettes are only practical for spring skiing

A short, fitted jacket might make your legs look longer, but does nothing to keep you warm

Outfit too restricting for vigorous movement

what it says about you

'I'm a fabulous skier, have an amazing figure and no one comes close to me on the slopes – in fact, I'm cold and very uncomfortable.'

on the slopes/ professional

✓ **Jacket is roomy enough for adventurous skiing but not too bulky**

Trousers are light- weight yet warm and waterproof

Outfit is practical and comfortable – just what a good skier needs

Goggles are the best non-steam on the market

what it says about you

'I know what I am doing, I'm not a flashy git. My style is in my impeccable slalom so I'm going to look great on the slopes anyway, whatever I wear.'

on the slopes/
beginner

✗ Wearing jeans to ski in might save money, but you'll be put off for life after a few hours of skiing in soggy clothes

However long your jacket is, it won't be enough to keep the snow out when worn with ordinary trousers

A fun hat might make it easier for the instructor to find you, but you'll be the laughing stock of the slopes

what it says about you

'I'm a prat who probably won't bother turning up to classes because I'll be too hung over. When I do, I'll take the piss, which will be funny at first but then get on everybody's tits.'

on the slopes/ beginner

✓ An all-in-one is the most comfortable thing to wear when you're learning to ski. No snow will get inside, you'll be warm all day. If you get too hot, you can control the input of cool air through the zip down your front

Dark colour means you'll be seen even in a blizzard.

Hat is warm and traditional

what it says about you

'I really want to learn to ski. I've borrowed this suit because I want to find out if I like whizzing headfirst down a mountain before I lash out the cash for my own outfit.'

winter holiday

on the slopes/poser

✗ A poser wants to look like how she thinks a professional might look if they had time to think about it

Once you know how to ski, the all-in-one, in a pastel tone, should be sent to the second-hand shop

Fabric is billowy and makes the bum twice the size

what it says about you
'I'm only here to be seen. The closest I'll get to any ice is in my mineral water.'

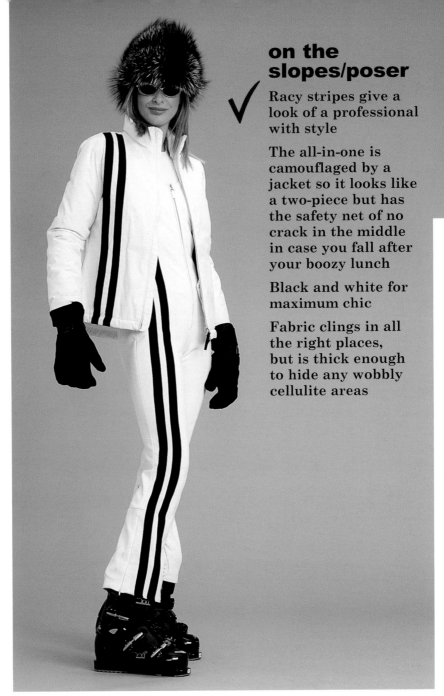

on the slopes/poser

✓ Racy stripes give a look of a professional with style

The all-in-one is camouflaged by a jacket so it looks like a two-piece but has the safety net of no crack in the middle in case you fall after your boozy lunch

Black and white for maximum chic

Fabric clings in all the right places, but is thick enough to hide any wobbly cellulite areas

what it says about you

'I'm a fair-weather skier and proud of it. Take me as I am and you'll love or hate me. If it's the latter, you won't spoil my holiday.'

après ski

X The evening will always be below freezing so even a fur gilet cannot be worn with nothing underneath

You're climbing mountains not the London social scene

Overdone hair should be left in the metropolis

winter holiday smart

what it says about you

'I'm more used to English country houses than ski resorts. I thought I should wear something warm... then I changed my mind.'

après ski

✓ Don't bother with fancy jewellery as it will always be too much

Winter white is the ultimate in mountain chic

Wearing hair down will prevent frostbitten ears

what it says about you

'I've had a great day on the slopes and I'm going to have an equally good evening. I know how to combine looking gorgeous with being warm and comfortable.'

8

après ski

✗ Even if you are staying in all evening, your PMT clothing will make you feel like a Nancy-no-friends

No woman should be seen in a man's sweat-shirt, even if it's the last piece of clothing on earth

Great shoes, but ruined by the way the socks are worn

what it says about you
'I don't want to appeal to anyone. I'm not worthy of human contact and should be kept in a cupboard under the stairs.'

après ski

✓ Sweatpants come in all shapes and sizes – so go for something slightly looser

Break up a matching top and trousers with a longer vest underneath. It's less Track and Field

Just the kind of thing you want to wear after a long day's sport

what it says about you

'Boy, I've had a truly tiring day off-piste. The snow was fabulous. This is all bullshit, but no one will know because my slick mufti clothes speak 'athlete'.'

après ski

X Wearing the trendiest look at a mountain resort will make you stand out as beginner

Very high heels turn roads into ice rinks

A mini with no tights looks simply ridiculous in such cold weather

what it says about you

'I've never been skiing before and I'm too stupid to realise that what I wear in my local club back home is neither practical nor appropriate.'

après ski

✓ Jeans are the best basic to build on

Jumpers can look very sexy if they are fitted and plunging

Long scarf keeps neck warm and looks cool

Boots are practically low but not too clumpy

what it says about you

'Come on, let's get a few schnapps down us, go out dancing and be up in time to take in a full day's skiing. Yes, I'm a girl who knows how to balance major fun with serious skiing.'

winter holiday/on the slopes/apres ski

where to shop

	£	££	£££
professional	Marks & Spencer, Lillywhites, Topshop, Zara, Designers at Debenhams, Mango, H & M, Miss Selfridge, River Island **Accessories** Freedom @ Topshop, Accessorize, Zara, Office, River Island	Billabong, Rip Curl, O'Neills, Quiksilver, Patagonia, Arcteryx, North Face, John Smedley, French Connection, Hobbs, Jigsaw, Karen Millen, Reiss, Uth **Accessories** Hobbs, LK Bennett, Jigsaw	Prada, Heidi Klein, Joseph, Karl Donoghue, Seven, Earl, Joie, Juicy Couture, Sass and Bide, Temperley, Brora, Ralph Lauren, Plein Sud, Dries van Noten **Accessories** Joseph, Karl Donoghue, Stephane Kélian, Sigerson Morrison
beginner	Marks & Spencer, Next Directory, H & M, Topshop, Dorothy Perkins, Oasis, Knickerbox, Toast **Accessories** Office, Dune	Killy, Snow + Rock, Lillywhiltes, Oakley, Killer Loop, Sweaty Betty, Puma, Nike, Calvin Klein Underwear, Wolford, Bodas **Accessories** Puma, Nike,	Helly Hansen, Nuala, Juicy Couture, Prada Sport, La Perla, Hogan, Tods **Accessories** Hogan, Tods
poser	Zara, Topshop, Warehouse, H & M, Oasis, River Island, Dorothy Perkins, Designers at Debenhams **Accessories** Freedom @ Topshop, Zara, Accessorize	Snow + Rock, Postcard, Jigsaw, Whistles, French Connection, John Smedley, Karen Millen **Accessories** Jigsaw, Whistles	Ralph Lauren, Escada, Chanel, Crystaux, Temperley, Joseph, Karl Donoghe, Ralph Lauren, Ann Louise Roswald, Prada, Alexander McQueen, Vivienne Westwood, Nicole Farhi, Donna Karen, Calvin Klein **Accessories** Joseph, Karl Donoghe, Erickson Beamon

winter holiday

- If your sunglasses are too big, the suntan marks after a hard day's skiing will drive you crazy. Take smaller, thirties-style, wraparound ones that still give protection, yet allow for a natural mark-free tan.

- Always cut your toenails before getting fitted for ski boots, otherwise the amount of pressure you put on them when skiing could make your toenails fall off

- When skiing in very cold conditions, it's far better to add more layers than wear heavy clothes. Layers provide more places for your body heat to be trapped

- If you suffer from bad circulation, don't forget to pack hand and foot warmers – found in any skiing or shooting shop

- A foot massage in the evening will stimulate tired muscles and prepare you for your ski boots the following day. Weleda do a fantastic arnica version you can also put in the bath

- If you are quite unfit or relatively new to skiing, take arnica in preparation for falls and tired muscles

- Apply sun protection liberally. Winter sun and wind can burn, even in January

- Take Optrex on the slopes for tired, hung-over or wind-damaged eyes

- Always have some tissues with you as so many loos don't have any

tips

partying Enjoying a party is as much about feeling smug in the knowledge that you look divine as it is about who you hang with and how much alcohol is consumed. The key is to forget the kind of people that are going to be there and focus on the type of event it is you've been invited to. Stick to what suits your shape and consider how smart you want to be. If you want to stand out from the crowd, it's easier to do so by over-dressing a bit. This doesn't mean raiding the kids dressing-up box. We are thinking more about glamour than fancy dress. Just because a bash is in the garden with food cooked on an open fire doesn't mean you have to forego style. Play it down with jeans, then ramp up the sex appeal. A subtle cleavage or peak of midriff will be enough to make you the centre of attention. Looking as though you were born at a film premiere or a black tie ball is what creates charisma. Trying too hard, being predictable ('she always looks like that') or not bothering at all are easy mistakes to make and a turn-off. Focus on your physical strengths, be true to your individuality and remember subdued sexuality is better than overexposure. You'll look great. Have a ball!

partying

9

winter

✗ If you buy only one evening dress a year, choosing velvet will only allow a winter outing

A feather boa should be kept for the cast of Moulin Rouge or fancy dress

Long black satin gloves show that you either have a problem with nail biting or live in another era

what it says about you

'I'm a loud show-off, who will blast your eardrums and empty the dance floor with my over-the-top antics.'

winter

✓ Satin is one of the most luxurious – yet sexy – fabrics to wear in the evening

The jacket brings glamour to a simple dress and makes an outfit more adaptable. If you arrive and find everyone is more casual – whisk it off

The shoes are elegant, yet unobtrusive. With an evening dress shoes should be seen but not heard

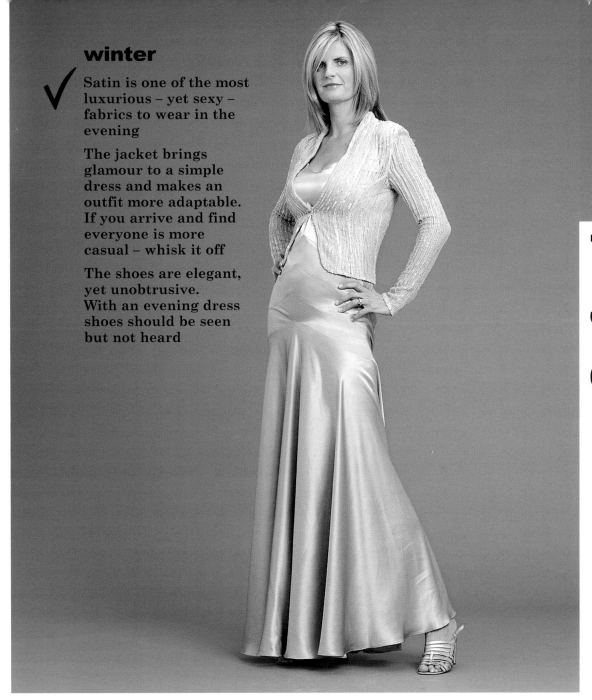

what it says about you

'I don't need to show off my tits and acres of leg to look sexy. I know that an understated, clinging number can be much more intriguing.'

winter

✗ Being too dressed up at your own dinner party can intimidate the guests and make them feel they should do the kitchen work

Tottering heels at home look like you are about to leave any minute

what it says about you

'I'm not really too at ease with all this entertaining and this is probably going to be a difficult evening for me as well as you.'

winter

✓ A gorgeous skirt with a simple top looks elegant yet informal

Shoes can be kitten, flat or kicked off

Long skirt or loose trousers are relaxed and lounge-proof

what it says about you

'I know how to be comfortable as well as looking good so I can relax and enjoy myself with friends without worrying about whether I'm creasing my clothes.'

winter

X Urban outfits should be unfussy – not too many frills and flounces

Black and white will encourage guests to keep asking you for a drink

If you use Carmen rollers in your hair, remember to brush out afterwards

what it says about you

'I've overdone my outfit to make up for my lack of charm and conversation. I'll probably need to rush to the loo every five minutes to check my frills and curls.'

winter

✓ **You can't go wrong with black if it suits you and if it doesn't, keep it as far from your face as possible**

Simple chic speaks volumes in terms of style

Make sure heels aren't too high for a standing event

what it says about you

'My clothes are understated, yet elegant and I'm confident that I look great without being overly formal. Nothing fussy – just perfection.'

summer

✗ Over-the-top sparkle doesn't compensate for a short length if the invitation is for long

Be careful with sequins as they can be very enlarging

They can also be very tacky if displayed en-masse

what it says about you
'Don't have a long frock so maybe if I wear something tight and showy everyone will be too busy admiring my bum to notice that I'm not dressed right.'

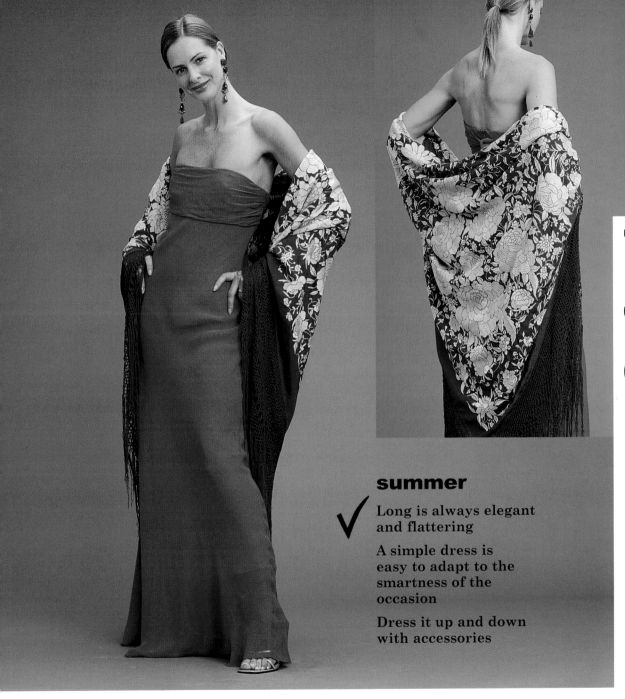

summer

✓ Long is always elegant
and flattering

A simple dress is
easy to adapt to the
smartness of the
occasion

Dress it up and down
with accessories

what it says about you

'I don't need to pile on the glitz. My dress may be plain
but the shawl is a showstopper and I know how to carry
it off with style.'

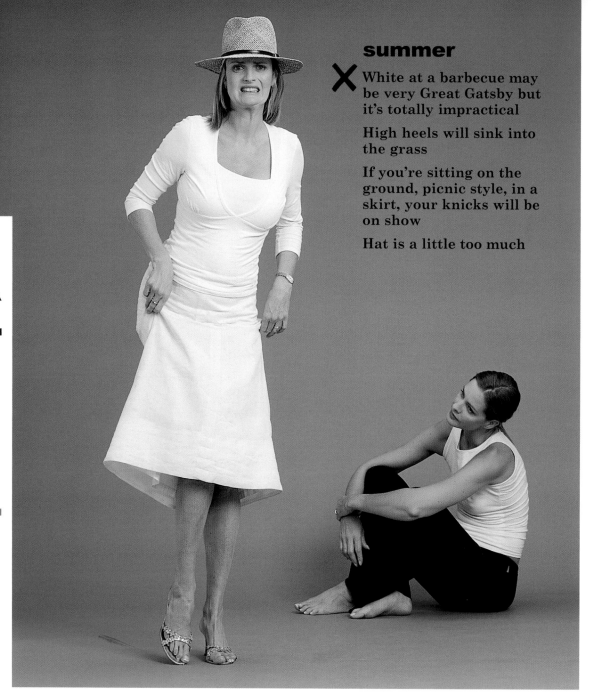

summer

✗ White at a barbecue may be very Great Gatsby but it's totally impractical

High heels will sink into the grass

If you're sitting on the ground, picnic style, in a skirt, your knicks will be on show

Hat is a little too much

what it says about you

'I don't really like being outdoors and I'm frightened of getting mud on my shoes so I don't think I'll enjoy myself or stay very long.'

summer

✓ Jeans allow for rough-and-ready outdoor treatment

Top could be the only thing seen if there's a crowd of guests so make sure it's pretty

Comfort is as much a factor as style

what it says about you

'I know how to look sexy but I'll still muck in and do my turn at the barbecue. And if get ketchup on my jeans… what the hell!'

summer

✗ Don't be fooled into thinking short equals sexy

Childish hairstyles are great...on children

Don't wear a trend unless it suits you – you'll be the laughing stock of the party rather than the envy of fellow guests

what it says about you
'I'm just a girlie at heart so if I wear girlie clothes no one will notice that I've, well... got a little older.'

summer

✓ If there isn't a trendy look you feel comfortable with, choose the colours and fabrics that are in

It's easier to be trendy and look good with separates

Separates also get more use as they can be worn with other things

what it says about you

'I always manage to look up to the minute – but in my own individual way. Well-chosen separates are the backbone of my wardrobe.'

partying/winter

	£	££	£££
smart	Zara, Monsoon, Topshop, Warehouse, H & M, Oasis, Designers at Debenhams, Mango **Accessories** Faith, Accessorize, Freedom @ Topshop, Bertie, Office, Dune, Designers at Debenhams, Mango	Karen Millen, LK Bennett, Jigsaw, Press & Bastyan, French Connection, Miliana T **Accessories** Karen Millen, LK Bennett, Pied à Terre, Kurt Geiger, Butler and Wilson, Agatha	Elspeth Gibson, Ben di Lisi, Temperley, Ralph Lauren, Calvin Klein, Alberta Ferretti, Gucci, Prada, Vivienne Westwood, Jean Paul Gaultier, Collette Dinnigan, Armani, John Galliano, Alexander McQueen, Valentino **Accessories** Gina, Gucci, Prada, Jimmy Choo, Manolo Blahnik, Judith Leiber, Jamin Puech
casual	Zara, Monsoon, H & M, Warehouse, Designers at Debenhams, Principles, Dorothy Perkins, Mango **Accessories** Accessorize, Designers at Debenhams Office, Faith, Dune, Freedom @ Topshop, Claire's Accessories	Jigsaw, Whistles, Karen Millen, Reiss, Uth, John Smedley, Michael Stars, Sara Berman, From Somewhere **Accessories** Jigsaw, Karen Millen, Pied à Terre, LK Bennett, Post Mistress	Marni, Temperley, Chloé, CXD, Brora, Ann Louise Roswald, Rozae Nichols, Ghost **Accessories** Marni, Sigerson Morrison, Stephane Kélian
trendy	Zara, Monsoon, Accessorize, H & M, Warehouse, Oasis, Topshop **Accessories** Zara, Accessorize, H & M, Warehouse, Designers at Debenhams, Office, Faith Dune, Oasis, Topshop, Mikey	Jigsaw, Karen Millen, Coast, French Connection **Accessories** Butler and Wilson, Agatha, LK Bennett, Kurt Geiger, Jigsaw, Coast, Post Mistress	Prada, Dolce and Gabbana, Roberto Cavalli, Temperley, Blumarine, Matthew Williamson, Chloé, Collette Dinnigan, Boyd, Virginia, Steinberg and Tolkien **Accessories** Sigerson Morrison, Gina, Jimmy Choo, Christian Louboutin, Jamin Puech, Erickson Beamon, Emma Hope

partying/summer

	£	££	£££
smart	Zara, Monsoon, Topshop, Warehouse, Oasis, H & M, Designers at Debenhams, **Accessories** Mikey, Freedom @ Topshop, Zara, Faith, Accessorize, Bertie	Karen Millen, Jigsaw, Press & Bastyan, French Connection, Holly, Whistles **Accessories** LK Bennett, Press & Bastyan, Pied à Terre, Kurt Geiger, Butler and Wilson, Agatha	Elspeth Gibson, Ben di Lisi, Temperley, Gina, Alberta Ferretti, Gucci, Prada, Armani, Vivienne Westwood, John Galliano **Accessories** Gina, Gucci, Prada, Jimmy Choo, Manolo Blahnik, Judith Leiber, Valentino, Erickson Beamon, Philip Treacy, Merola
casual	Topshop, Warehouse, Oasis, Gap, H & M, Zara, Miss Selfridge, Monsoon, Designers at Debenhams, Mango, Principles, River Island, Kookai, Morgan, Pink Soda **Accessories** Accessorize, Unique, Freedom @ Topshop	Whistles, French Connection, Studd, Saltwater, Tata Naka, Miliana T, French Connection, Holly, Martin Kidman, Shirin Guild, Jigsaw **Accessories** Whistles, Karen Millen, LK Bennett, Pied à Terre, Pebble, Urban Outfitters,	Betsy Johnson, Cacharel, House of Jazz, Marni, Temperley, Seven, Sass and Bide, Paper Denim Cloth, Joie, Marc Jacobs, Sybil Slanislaus, Dosa, Zakee Shariff **Accessories** Sigerson Morrison, Scorah Patullo, Pippa Small, Me and Ro, Zilo, Erickson Beamon
trendy	Monsoon, Oasis, H & M, Zara, Topshop, Designers at Debenhams, Warehouse, New Look, Office, Dune, Pink Soda, Kal Kaur Rai **Accessories** Faith, Oasis, H & M, Zara, Office, Dune	Miliana T, Whistles, French Connection, Reiss, Michael Stars, Holly **Accessories** Pied à Terre, Whistles, Post Mistress, Lola Rose, Agatha, Butler and Wilson, Pebble	Virginia, Joseph, Narcisco Rodriguez, Louis Vuitton, Missoni, Megan Park, Marc Jacobs, Fendi, Etro, Blumarine, Temperley **Accessories** Christian Louboutin, Sigerson Morrison, Louis Vuitton, Pippa Small, Me and Ro

partying

- Cut down make-up to fit into an evening bag and yet retain all your requirements. For instance, sharpen down pencils – it's not a waste, you'll always lose them before they're ground down – and put loose powder in a small MAC powder container

- If you are in for a long night, use a make-up primer under your foundation. Check out Laura Mercier, Nars, Vincent Longo Water Canvas

- Don't take such a big bag that you end up having to dance around it all evening

- Think whether your shoes will carry you through the night?

- If you're wearing a smart evening outfit, don't ruin it with a daytime watch

- Are you likely to get your period? Take tampax

- If you're planning on getting smashed, think about heel height – and falling over

- Eat a few almonds to line an empty stomach if you're going to drink a lot before dinner

- Mints for the sexy snog

- If you're going to a big event in winter, consider taking a shawl instead of a heavy coat so you can avoid the coat check queue in and out

- Do make sure you've got enough money for a cab if things don't go to plan

underwear Are you aware that three-quarters of you are wearing the wrong-sized bra. Look down. Do your tits give off a vibe of wanting to escape? Are they sneaking over the top of the lace? Turn around. Do you see your bra straps digging furrows in your back and is there a feeling of a restraining order being imposed upon your udders? Keeping your eyes downcast, do you see the outline of pretty lace through your T-shirt? Or worse, has the sexy black lace turned dirty grey when covered with a pale top? Hmm. Now, it's time to get off your arse to check the state of your butt in a full-length mirror. How many cheeks do you see? Two or four? Would an onlooker be aware that you prefer knickers to g-strings? And talking of g-strings, when you bend over to pick up a toy or a boy, does a rather nasty worn-out Y appear above the waistband? Swivel to the side. How does your tummy look? Ready to deliver a litter or dough-like with a full-blown yeast infection? If any of the above applies to your clothed anatomy, waste no time in correcting the problem. What's the point of pouring time and effort into cool looks when your underwear is total shit?

underwear

10

problem/flabby tummy

X Ask all but flat-stomached freaks what they detest most about their bodies and the unanimous cry will be 'my bloody tummy'. A flabby tummy is the most hated defect among women

what's the problem?

'The tummy is an impossible area to get back into shape after having kids and the bane of those who like a carb fix from time to time. If you're not going to resort to surgery, then we advise the use of radical underwear.'

solution

✓ Magic knickers create smooth, sleek lines enabling you to wear figure-hugging clothes that you might have banned from your life for years

what to do

'Wear magic knickers. They may not eradicate tummy bulges all together, but they will make soft flesh firm and wobble-free and give the tum an instant iron-out.'

problem/ visible g-string

✗ You don't think of the impact your thong might have when you bend or crouch down or when your jeans slither down your hips

underwear

what's the problem?

'Visible thongs are really only a problem for those partial to hipster trousers and low-slung waistbands. But we are here to tell you a crusty, worn-out cheesecutter is not a pretty sight.'

solution

✓ If you're going to flash your knickers, make sure they're worth looking at rather than a barren triangle of grubby nylon

underwear

what to do
'Luckily there are people who care enough about our butts. These Guardians of the Rear have come up with prettily decorated thongs that flash sequined butterflies and the like.'

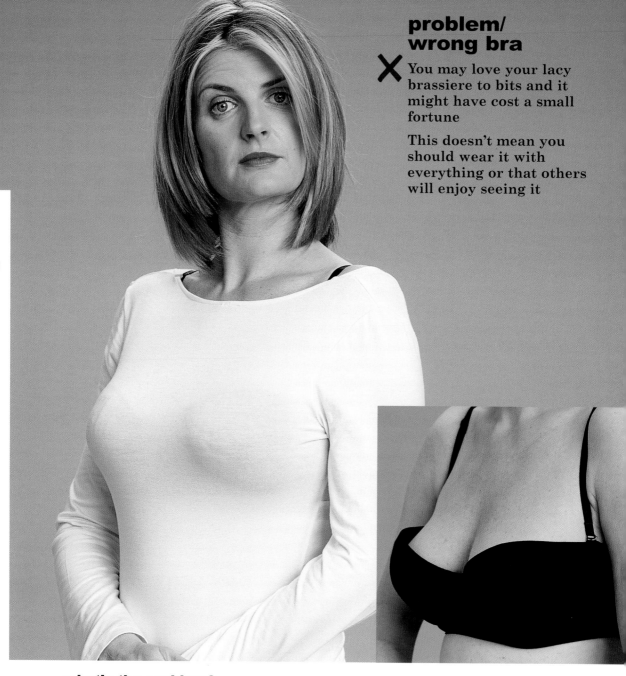

problem/ wrong bra

X You may love your lacy brassiere to bits and it might have cost a small fortune

This doesn't mean you should wear it with everything or that others will enjoy seeing it

what's the problem?

'The wrong bra can rough up your pale or smooth-fitting tops. It is such a shame to ruin the possibility of a smart clean line with a black or over-adorned bra.'

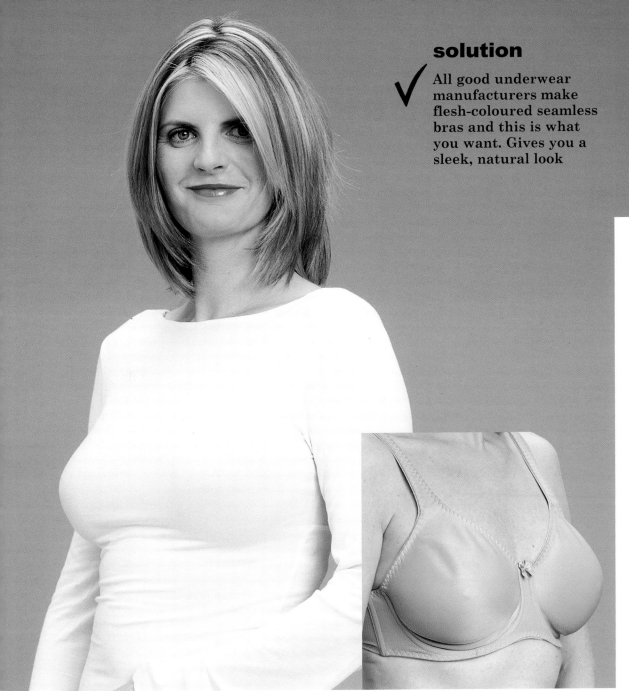

solution

✓ All good underwear manufacturers make flesh-coloured seamless bras and this is what you want. Gives you a sleek, natural look

what to do

'Be sure to have your bra properly fitted so that your tits don't spill out the top and the straps don't dig into the shoulders or back.'

underwear

	£	££	£££
sexy	Topshop, H & M, Miss Selfridge, Zara, Pretty Polly	Cosabella, Wild Hearts @ Marks and Spencer, Elle MacPherson Intimates, Love Kylie, Calvin Klein, Fantasie	Damaris, Agent Provocateur, La Perla, Myla, Sabia Rosa, Collette Dinnigan, Donna Karan
athletic	Maidenform @ Debenhams, Gap Body, Marks & Spencer, Next, Presence at Debenhams, H & M, Knickerbox	Bodas, Lejaby, Chantelle, Warners, Wolford, DKNY, Freya, Charnos, Elle McPherson, Bodas, Jigsaw, Calvin Klein	Magic Knickers, La Perla, Rigby and Pellar, La Perla, Hanro

underwear

- Always make sure you have your bits done

- If you are wearing tight trousers don't wear bikini knickers – they will cut your bum cheeks in half

- Bridget Jones knickers won't get you laid, but magic knickers will keep your tum in

- Breasts can change size. Keep getting your size checked and get a bra that fits

- If you are flat chested but find yourself in need of a flesh-coloured bra to wear under a skimpy outfit, cut up a pair of flesh-coloured tights above the gusset, make it into a bandeau and and slip it on like a bra

- If you're wearing a calf-length skirt, don't take the risk of wearing pop socks – they will be seen

- If you're going out in the evening and intend to have bare legs, don't wear pop socks during the day as the marks won't have gone

- If you have to wear tights with sandals make sure the toe is seamless

- If you're going to wear a backless dress in the evening, be aware of the tightness of your bra during the day. Any marks will show later

- Don't machine-wash an under-wired bra because the plastic bobble at the end will melt, allowing the sharp wiring to poke through the fabric

Accessorize 020 7313 3000
Adidas 0870 240 4204
Agatha 020 7495 2779
Agent Provocateur 020 7927 6999
Alberta Ferretti 020 7235 2349
Alexander McQueen 020 7278 4333
Allegra Hicks 020 7589 2323
Amanda & Odi @ Heidi Klein
Ann Demeulemeester @ Harvey Nichols,
  Selfridges
Ann Louise Roswald 020 7250 1583
Anya Hindmarch 020 7838 9177
Arcteryx @ Snow + Rock
Aristoc 01773 525 520
Armani 020 7823 8818

Balenciaga @ Harvey Nichols, Selfridges
Basia Zarzycka 020 7730 1660
Bella Freud for Jaeger 020 7200 2990
Ben di Lisi 020 7730 2994
Benetton 020 7331 1433
Bertie 020 7493 5033
Betsy Johnson 020 7591 0005
Betty Jackson 020 7602 6023
Billabong @ Selfridges
Billy Bag 020 7723 0427
Birkenstock 0800 132 194
Blumarine 020 74934872
Bodas 0870 333 0411
Boden 0845 357 5000
Boss by Hugo Boss 020 7534 2700
Bottega Veneta 020 7838 9394
Boyd 020 7730 3939
Brora 020 7736 9944
Browns 020 7514 0016
Browns Focus 020 7514 0063
Buba @ Selfridges
Burberry London 07000 785676
Butler and Wilson 020 7409 8686

Cacharel 020 7631 3157
Calvin Klein 020 7491 9696
Cath Kidston 020 7221 4000
Celine 020 7297 4999
Chanel 020 7493 3836
Chantelle @ Fenwick, John Lewis
Charnos 0115 850 8000
Chloé 020 7823 5348
Christian Dior 020 77235 1357
Christian Louboutin 020 7823 2234
CK Calvin Klein 020 7259 6011
Claire's Accessories 0121 682 8000
Coast 020 7490 9999
Coccinelle 020 7924 6180

Coco De Mer 020 7836 8882
Collette Dinnigan 020 7589 8897
Cosabella @ Fenwick, Harrods, Liberty,
  Selfridges
The Cross 020 7727 6760
Crystal @ Selfridges
CXD @ Selfridges

Damaris @ Harvey Nichols
Day Birger et Mikkelsen 020 7267 8822
Debenhams 020 7408 4444
Diane Von Furstenberg 020 7838 0703
Diesel 020 7833 2255
Dior by Galliano 020 7235 1357
DKNY 020 499 6238
Dolce and Gabbana 020 7201 0980
Dollargrand 020 7431 2756
Donna Karan 020 7495 3100
Dorothy Perkins 0870 731 8285
Dosa @ Browns
Dries van Noten @ Harvey Nichols, Liberty
Dune 020 7258 3605

Earl Jean 020 7727 9903
East 0973 832302
Elle McPherson @ Selfridges
Elspeth Gibson 020 7226 0770
Emma Hope 020 7792 7800
Erickson Beamon 020 7259 0202
Escada 020 7580 6066
Etro 020 7495 5767

Faith 0800 289 297
Fantasie 01536 764336
Fenwick 020 7629 9161
Florence and Fred @ Tesco 0800 505555
FootPrints Swimwear 01536 764 334
Frankie B @ Harvey Nichols, Selfridges
Fred Bare @ Harvey Nichols, Selfridges
Freedom @ Topshop
Free Lance (Paris) 00 33 2 51 66 36 36
French Connection 020 7399 7200
Freya @ Selfridges
From Somewhere 020 8743 7061
FrostFrench 020 7272 3090
Furla 020 7730 2888

Gabriella Ligenza 020 7730 2200
Gap 0800 427 789
George @ Asda 0500 100 055
Gharani Strok 020 8749 5909
Ghost @ Liberty, Selfridges
Gina 020 7409 7090
Givenchy 020 7629 1234

Gucci 020 7629 2716

H&M 020 7323 2211
Harrods 020 7730 1234
Harvey Nichols 0870 873 3833
Heidi Klein 020 7243 5665
Helly Hansen 0115 960 8797
Helmut Lang @ Harvey Nichols, Selfridges
Hermès 020 7499 8856
Hobbs 020 7586 5550
Hogan 020 7546 1888
House of Jazz 020 8533 5051

Inside Out @ Question Air 020 7221 8163
J&M Davidson 020 7313 9532
The Jacksons 020 7792 8336
Jade Jagger @ Browns Focus
Jaeger 020 7200 2990
Jamin Puech @ Selfridges
Jasper Conran 020 7384 0800
Jean-Paul Gaultier 020 7584 4648
Jigsaw 020 7491 4484
Jimmy Choo 020 7591 7000
J Maskrey 020 7613 2909
John Galliano @ Harrods
John Lewis 08456 049049
Johnny Loves Rosie 020 7247 1496
John Smedley 0800 028 6792
Joie @ Selfridges
Jones the Bootmaker 0800 163 519
Joseph 020 7590 6200
Judith Leiber @ Harrods
Juicy Couture 020 7235 5000

Kal Kaur Rai @ Topshop
Karen Millen 01622 664 032
Karl Donoghue 020 7378 6650
Kate Kuba 020 8444 1227
Kate Spade @ Harrods
Kenzo 020 7235 4021
Killer Loop @ Selfridges
Killy 020 8968 2300
Knickerbox 0845 456 2343
Koh Samui 020 7240 4280/020 7838 9292
Kookai 020 7368 6900
Kurt Geiger 020 7546 1888

La Perla 020 7245 0527
Lara Bohnic @ Harvey Nichols
La Redoute 0500 777 777
Laura Ashley 0870 562 2116
Laura Mercier 020 7355 1727
Lejaby @ Harvey Nichols
Liberty 020 7734 1234

Lillywhites 0870 333 9600
Liza Bruce 020 7235 8423
L K Bennett 020 7643 0027
Lola Rose @ Fenwick
Louis Vuitton 020 7399 4050
Love Kylie @ Selfridges
Luella at Mulberry 020 7491 4430
Luisa Beccaria @ The Cross
Lulu Guinness 020 7823 4828

MAC 020 7534 9686
Magic Knickers 020 7259 6620
Maharishi 020 7836 3860
Maidenform @ Debenhams
Mambo 020 7384 4403
Mango 01322 624 704
Manolo Blahnik 020 7352 3863
Marc Jacobs @ A la Mode 020 7730 7180
Marc by Marc Jacobs 020 7235 5000
Maria Grachvogel 020 7245 9331
Marilyn Moore @ Fenwick
Marks & Spencer 020 7268 1234
Marni 0207 235 1991
Martin Kidman @ Matches
Matches 020 8542 9416
Matthew Williamson 020 7637 4600
Me and Ro @ Harrods, Harvey Nichols,
    Liberty, Selfridges
Megan Park 020 7739 5828
Melissa Odabash@ Heidi Klein
Merola 020 7351 9338
Michael Kors @ Harvey Nichols
Michael Stars @ Whistles
Mikey 020 7437 1101
Miliana T @ The Cross
Mimi 020 7349 9699
Missoni A La Mode 020 7730 7180
Miss Selfridge 0800 915 9900
Miss Sixty 020 7836 3789
Miu Miu 020 7409 0900
Monsoon 020 7313 3000
Morgan 0800 731 4942
Moschino 0207 318 0555
Mossie @ Topshop
Mulberry 020 7491 4430

Naf Naf @ Selfridges
Narciso Rodriguez @ Harvey Nichols
Nars @ Space NK
New Look 01305 765 000
Next 08702 435 435
Nicole Farhi 020 7499 8368
Niketown 020 7612 0800
Nine West 020 7629 3875

Nougat 020 7323 2222
North Face 020 7240 9577
Nuala @ Selfridges

Oakley @ Harvey Nichols
Oasis 01865 881 986
Office 020 7566 3070
Ollie & Nic @ Topshop
O'Neill 020 7240 9430
Orla Kiely 020 7585 3322

Paper Denim Cloth @ Harvey Nichols,
    Selfridges
Patagonia @ Selfridges
Patch NYC @ Willma 020 8960 7296
Patrick Cox 020 7730 8886
Paul and Joe 020 7243 5510
Paul Smith Women 020 7379 7133
Paule Ka 020 7647 4455
Pebble 020 7262 1775
Peekaboo @ Topshop
Philip Treacy 020 7730 3992
Pied à Terre 020 7380 3800
Pink Soda 020 7636 9001
Pippa Small @ The Cross
Plein Sud 020 7584 8295
Polo Ralph Lauren 020 7535 4600
Portobello Market, Fridays and Saturdays
    London W11
Post Mistress @ Office 020 7379 4040
Prada 020 7647 5000
Prada Sport 020 7647 5000
Presence at Debenhams
Press & Bastyan 020 7491 0597
Pretty Polly 01773 525520
Princess Tam Tam @ Selfridges
Principles 0870 122 8802
Pringle 0800 360 200
Pucci 020 7287 8990
Puma 020 7439 0221
Quiksilver 020 7436 6800

Rachel Robarts @ The Cross
Ralph Lauren 020 75354600
Ravel 01458 843 222
Red Hot @ Selfridges
Reiss 020 7225 4900
Rigby and Peller 020 7491 2200
Rip Curl @ Selfridges
River Island 020 8991 4759
Roberto Cavalli @ Harvey Nichols,
    Selfridges
Roland Mouret 020 7376 5762
Ronit Zilkha 020 7499 3707

Rozae Nichols @ Harvey Nichols
Russell & Bromley 020 7629 6903
Saltwater @ Selfridges
Sara Berman 020 7734 1234
Sass and Bide @ Browns, Harvey Nichols
Scholl 0870 729 0222
Scorah Patullo 020 7792 0100
Seafolly 020 7629 9161
Selfridges 08708 377 377
Seven @ Selfridges
Shirin Guild @ Liberty
Sigerson Morrison 020 7229 8465
Silhouette 020 8889 9997
Snow + Rock 01932 570070
Solange Azagury-Partridge 020 7792 0197
Space NK 0870 169 9999
Sportmax 020 7287 3434
Steinberg and Tolkien 020 7376 3660
Stella McCartney 020 7898 3000
Stephane Kélian 020 7235 9459
St Tropez 0115 983 6363
Studd 020 7563 7391
Swarovski 01737 856 812
Sweaty Betty 0800 169 3889
Sybil Stanislaus @ Ajanta 020 7235 1572

Tata Naka @ Selfridges
Temperley 020 7229 7957
Thomas Pink 020 7498 3882
Toast 0870 240 5200
Tods 020 7235 1321
Topshop 0800 731 8284

Ungaro 020 7629 0550
Urban Outfitters 020 7761 1001
Uth 020 7734 7261
Valentino 020 7235 5855
Vanessa Bruno @ The Cross
Versace 020 7499 1862
Vincent Longo 01252 741600
Virginia 020 7727 9908
Vivienne Westwood 020 7924 4747
Wallis 0800 915 9901
Warehouse 0870 122 8813
Warners 0191 259 6800
West Village @ Selfridges
Whistles 020 7487 4484
Wolford 020 7499 2549
Wright and Teague 020 7629 2777

YSL 020 7493 1800)
Zakee Shariff 0870 837 7377
Zara 020 7534 9500
Zilo @ Erickson Beamon

VERSACE/AVEDON